Boy Wander

A Coming of Age Memoir

JOBERT E. ABUEVA

RATTLING GOOD YARNS
PRESS

Rattling Good Yarns Press
33490 Date Palm Drive 3065
Cathedral City CA 92235
USA
www.rattlinggoodyarns.com

Library of Congress Control Number: 2022950888
ISBN: 978-1-955826-27-3

First Edition

To Tatay and Mommy, in loving memory

Chapters

Author's Note

The challenge of remembering faraway times and places was top of mind throughout this writing journey. I own up to any and all incorrections and inconsistencies, though the events within are what transpired to the best of my recollection.

Some names and identifying features have been changed to protect individuals' identities though each and every person mentioned is real.

And there's no denying that the truth has set me free.

"He who does not know how to look back at where he came from will never get to his destination."

~Jose Rizal, Philippines National Hero

Prologue

Manila, 1970

Click.

I turned around and saw him lock the door. We seemed to cross paths here often, our bladders synched to the same stopwatch. But this time was different: the extra rattling of the doorknob in his hand to make sure no one could get in accompanied by his plastic grin and crooked teeth, neither of which I had seen him sport before. I returned a half-smile and took a full step back, a chess piece in retreat.

His coffee eyes were framed in silver square glasses, and he had a scratchy mustache and short brown hair. This was the face that stood by the filing cabinet and sat at the typewriter in Tatay's office building. This was the face that cheerfully asked if I would like a Coke while I waited for Tatay's return from his lectures across campus. But with every deliberate step he took toward me, this was a face that became less and less familiar.

I bumped up against a stall. I was still. He stretched his left arm and combed his twig fingers through my hair. I closed my eyes and tilted my head, following the slow random motion of his moist pulsating palm over my face and around my neck. The urinal stench, sharp as the air whenever we drove by the squatter slums, made me want to hold my breath. Instead, I let out a faint purr.

He wrapped his hand around my waist and guided it toward his Buddha belly. Then he gripped my wrist. I tried to tug away but was unable to do so. His black polyester pants were slick as the negatives of a Kodak Instamatic. He hastily unzipped and reached inside to release what was brown and pink. He made me grab it and had me pull and push repeatedly. It smelled like Elmer's Glue. Then he let go, but I was still pushing and pulling in a rhythm all my own.

"Yes, just like that," he said.

It was a rubber band. It was a crayon. It was a ruler. I snapped my eyes up at him, but his crooked teeth stared back at me.

I pinched my eyes as he reached for the belt buckle of my khaki shorts. He brushed my crotch. He raised goosebumps as he rubbed me. I wanted to yelp, leap, flee. But I also wanted to see where this was all going. An electric current was running from ear to ear. I needed to say something. Do something. Anything. Right then and there.

"Please, may I go?"

My heart was the rhythm of bongo drums. He shushed me with a finger over his pursed lips and took several steps back. He was hurrying up, pushing and pulling. He had a serpent in his hands. He convulsed and grunted, grew louder and louder. All of a sudden, his hand and voice froze. A milky arc gushed over the honeycomb tiling and landed directly in front of me, a streak of goo. He was breathing as if he was dying. Smaller arcs. Smaller streaks.

I stared at the floor, then at his face which was no longer crumpled origami. With his pants and Jockeys still around his ankles, he penguined over to the sink. But not before he reached down into his pocket and raised up to my face a silver fifty centavo coin, a communion host that I was about to receive.

"Go buy yourself a soft drink. You deserve it."

I did not spend the money. I tucked it in my shoe, where my left sock met its sole, so no one would know I had it or ask how I acquired it.

Tatay, on the drive home, was whistling to Vivaldi's *Four Seasons* on the radio. Spring. Summer. Beginning of autumn. He did not ask me how my day went. I did not want him to. I would not have known where to start, even if I had to lie. I could not even tell how I felt about his not being in his office. Would it have mattered?

I excused myself as Mommy put out the last dish of string beans on the table, and we were about to thank God for this day and ask him to bless the food that we were about to receive.

I just wanted to be in bed and replay the afternoon over and over, projecting every move on my mind's movie screen. The coin laid beneath my pillow, as if it was left by the tooth fairy. There was this prickling sensation in the pit of my stomach and across my six-year-old chest. The yo-yo of good and bad.

I had excavated this fragment of memory from the ruins of my childhood, evidence of when this "best little boy in the world" crossed the line. To be not just the son of an academic and diplomat. Or Mommy's golden boy. Let alone a TV personality, the ambitious high school BMOC being groomed for greatness.

I had taken the first step in a lifelong path to discovering who I really was.

Awakening

Jobert aged 3

1
Tale of Two Kitchens

Antipolo, 1970-1971

When it came to our new home and its two kitchens, no one questioned Mommy's logic. Clean tasks were reserved for the clean kitchen and dirty ones relegated to the dirty kitchen. And she was sole arbiter.

The kitchens stood on opposite ends of the house. Even though we could cut through the dining and living rooms to get from one to the other, Mommy and the maids slunk through the side doors that wrapped around through the garage or open-air porch. Guests never saw or smelled any trace of cooking or cleaning up, yet everything had to look like it occurred in the clean kitchen. The illusion eluded them. And even when it was just our immediate family seated at the table, Mommy served dinner through the clean kitchen's entranceway, her Arc de Triomphe, when she could have easily taken the easy way in and out.

But the dirty kitchen was the central nervous system of our home. Though it was bathed in white tile and fluorescent lighting, and often reeking of Lysol, someone was always busy gutting fish, chopping vegetables, frying rice, or ironing a shirt. I sometimes sat in there after school with our two yayas and two maids isolating inedible black grains of rice from the day's ration so I could listen in on their juicy chismis.

With the transistor radio blaring Filipino soap operas and confessional talk shows, they argued over leading men they would die for as well as the quality of advice being dished to women raped by their bosses or brothers. They loved to laugh until they fell to the floor, tears streaming down their cheeks, palms slapping the tile, and insults and names darting across the room—usually "gaga," "bruha," "aswang," or some variation on the word "witch." They used phrases I was certain Mommy would have washed out their mouths with bars of Ajax for. I preferred sitting among our help to playing with children down the street.

I felt a comfort and bliss among these women I did not necessarily feel with family. I laughed as hard as they did. I was one with them in our circle of silliness. But as soon as Mommy returned from running errands, her car's horn tooting up the hill, I scurried up to my room to watch *Bugs Bunny* or *Popeye* or *My Favorite Martian*. Anything but be caught loitering in the dirty kitchen. Over time, I would come to accept the reality of our class differences as perhaps every Filipino child in a middle to upper class family did. I was a boy being groomed to expectations and destined to land somewhere good in life. They were merely gossiping girls, trying not to get pregnant by the male gardeners and guardsmen of the subdivision. The highlight of their month was a day off to go into town and mail their salaries in crumpled envelopes back to their respective families in the provinces.

The help's quarters opened into the dirty kitchen, where the soap-white GE washing machine sat between its companion dryer and a sink where an elephant trunk-like hose spewed out and drained water after the rinse cycle. Mommy supervised the lavendera on weekends, preferring to hand-wash and line-dry, saving on electricity as well as salvaging fabrics from the spinning and gurgling of the motorized monsters.

I donned each day's attire, wondering whether, like a hound, Mommy could sniff what my day had been like. When the man in Tatay's office had me push and pull on his penis in the locked bathroom that first time, and the two more times thereafter, I shuddered at the thought of her smelling him on my clothes, let alone on me. I thought Mommy and all other mothers were smart and sharp that way.

It was July. The year prior we had moved out of faculty housing at the University of the Philippines and into Beverly Hills, a residential enclave in the hills east of Manila in the town of Antipolo, known for roasted cashews, sticky rice-filled banana leaf suman, and the shrine that housed Our Lady of Good Voyage. We technically straddled two municipalities, Taytay and Antipolo, though we paid taxes to and attended Mass in Antipolo. I liked the fact that we could step back and forth across an imaginary borderline between towns several times a day. The winding roads were constantly overrun with pilgrims as anyone travelling abroad made a point of coming here, which led me to believe the land around us was sacred. This left me more terrified than blessed, fearful that the Virgin Mary, like in Lourdes and Fatima, could appear atop a nearby hill, or on the wishbone limbs of any one of our three mango trees.

We were at the table, dining on deep-fried fish heads, squash, rice, and chicken consommé made from Knorr bouillon cube concentrates when Tatay cleared his throat.

"I'll be on a visiting professorship at Yale starting next month," he said.

I had no idea where Yale was at the time and continued to chew. Mommy let out a small sigh and spun the lazy Susan, letting it stop on its own like a roulette wheel. She won squash.

"It'll be for two semesters in Connecticut, in the States," he added.

Oh, the States. It felt so far away. He would be leaving just three years since we returned from Brooklyn where he had been a visiting professor at CUNY and we had lived in Flatbush for an academic year. But then Baby Ruths, Snickers, and M&Ms as well as fat cans of Coke, 7UP, and Dr. Pepper filled my head like the store shelves of Clark Air Base near Angeles City and Subic Naval Base in Olongapo, strategic American outposts of an ongoing war across the South China Sea. It was always a treat when a family friend said something they brought was from the PX. And now Tatay could bring a luggage full of everything back direct from America.

"Tatay, how long?" I asked.

"Nine months, Job."

It did not seem like a long time until I counted each month aloud on the peaks and valleys of my knuckled fist. He would be gone for Christmas. And New Year's. And my seventh birthday in March.

"And Lanelle will be coming with me."

I sat up as if the fish I'd eaten had bitten me. Lanelle, my older sister, now fourteen, grew a grin as wide as a slice of watermelon. She had known she was going. I could see it in the way she threw back her shoulders as she put a spoonful of Rocky Road into her mouth and slid the spoon out and up from between her pursed lips in slow motion. I did not like it that she knew before the rest of us did. I did not like secrets if I wasn't a part of them.

"Can I go, too?"

"You just entered prep school at Ateneo," Mommy said, pleased I was attending the Jesuit-run school where she happened to work in personnel administration on the college side of the same campus. "You, Rossana, Jonas and I will stay here toge—"

"You'll be the man of the house while I'm gone," said Tatay.

I perked up at the thought of bossing around my younger sister and brother, proving that I could think and act mature for a six-year-old. Rossana, three and a half, and Jonas, two and a half, did not seem to understand what was going on.

But they eventually did and made their feelings clear the day Tatay and Lanelle departed.

"I hate you, Tatay. I hate you. I hate you," Rossana wailed while Jonas whimpered in the middle of the departure area of Manila International Airport.

I repeated her words inside my head until the syllables broke down into senseless sounds. I, too, hated him. Why was he going away for so long? Why now? Why Lanelle and not me? Mommy lifted my stubborn arm to wave goodbye from the observation deck as they, like ants, walked the tarmac and up the boarding stairs onto a Pan Am Boeing 707.

The night before when I had pretended to be asleep in my bed, facing the wall, Tatay brushed my hair with his warm fingers before kissing my forehead. At first I did not want to tell or ask him anything about what was happening to me or what I was feeling about the man in his office bathroom. But a part of me thought, that he, a man, might understand what was going on. He always seemed to listen, with his hands clasped and index fingers forming a church steeple under his nose, before he spoke in his calming voice. Telling Mommy would be tricky, like climbing a volcano. And besides, if he could keep a secret with Lanelle, he certainly could keep one with me. Alas, I never approached him. I thought I would be blamed for allowing the man to do what he did to me, and I would be punished and locked in my room for the rest of my life.

The car radio, usually on, was not during the drive home from the airport. Rossana and Jonas were asleep in the backseat. I looked up to Mommy on my left. She was silent, slightly hunched over the wheel, focused on the road. Her face had shriveled into a Sun-Maid raisin. The last time I had seen her like this was a year earlier when we drove back home at the break of dawn after she had taken me to a faith healer. She had paid a female attendant a wad of peso bills before he laid his sandpaper hands on my face to pray cure my lazy left eye.

I did not know how to comfort her the way Tatay could when she was sad or sick. I had too many of my own thoughts to contend with. One thing I knew for sure: I did not want to be "the man of the house," whatever that was.

Jonas and I shared a bedroom. We each had a matching desk built into the wall, shelving, side table, and closet. Lanelle and Rossana's room mirrored ours. Both rooms had doors, one blue and one pink, leading into the same bathroom. We had sibling symmetry: girl, boy, girl, boy. We were an even six in a family that was not too big, not too small. But with Tatay and Lanelle in America, and Rossana sleeping in Mommy's room at night, everything felt lopsided.

Collie, my yaya, had followed us to Beverly Hills and was joined by another yaya, Marina, who was more Rossana's and Jonas's. She and Collie acted as if they were tethered to every one of us, tripping over each other as they reacted to our every whim, wish, or pair of wet shorts. They were Mommy's sergeants, and their priority was not to anger her or else risk being thrown out of the house as Mommy had done with the gardener and one of the maids a few weeks after Tatay and Lanelle had left. According to them, the two had been caught doing something they were not supposed to behind the water tank. Did this have something to do with getting pregnant?

Our yayas and maid were always up before we were in the morning. Sometimes I woke to the sound of trembling stacks of porcelain plates in transit between both kitchens, downstairs in the dark. Soon after, Mommy emerged from her bedroom, and the first, pale artificial light of day switched on along the corridor that connected our bedrooms.

The yayas cajoled us out of bed with a sing-songy, "time for school," and "time for sunshine." Then they washed the sleep out of our faces with warm, wet cloths before putting on our school uniforms, and then feeding us Frosted Flakes or chocolate porridge champorado with condensed milk, as well as a glass of warm powdered milk and chilled papaya juice. When Mommy called out that it was time to go, they carried our school bags into the Volkswagen station wagon my parents shipped back from our camping expedition in Germany on the way back from Brooklyn. Mommy drove us to school before heading to work. As she revved up the engine and reversed the car out of the lone garage and, hence, home on Dahlia Drive, she shouted the day's task list out the window to the household troops in Tagalog and mostly to Collie, who then divvied up the duties amongst them.

"Wax the floors upstairs, finish cutting the grass, buy more rice at the market, shake out the curtains." She barked orders even as the car rolled down the street.

When we returned in the afternoon, Rossana, Jonas, and I watched TV, took a bath and put on our pajamas while Mommy took a nap. I hardly spent time anymore in the dirty kitchen with the girls. Mommy joined us for dinner, then disappeared into the dirty kitchen and yelled at one or more of the girls, likely for a poorly executed task, before tucking us in bed by nine.

Mommy was unable to keep Tatay from leaving us, but she could control the appearance of our home, if not the behavior of those who lived in it. And like the maid and yayas, the new gardener and lavendera, and even Rossana and Jonas, I thought it best to blend into the day's routine and not upset Mommy.

Since I had seen and felt the man's penis bloat up those few times in the locked bathroom, I wanted to see if I could get mine to do the same. It was not until right after Tatay was gone that, whenever I went to the bathroom to pee or poop, I double checked that the doors were locked, closed the toilet lid, and sat on it with my shorts and briefs still shucked around my ankles. I started pushing and pulling on my fleshy penis with my left hand.

Nothing happened no matter how fast I pushed and pulled on it. I made at least one attempt each day for weeks. I started talking to my penis. "Do something, now." I even asked God to intervene. I could not stay too long, though. Collie sometimes knocked on the door and asked if I was not feeling well. I faked a cough or two in response and said I was almost done.

Tatay and Lanelle had been gone for three or four months. Mommy was with us but was caught up in her own routine and melancholy and exhaustion. Her eyes seemed to search for someone or something beyond us every time she spoke.

One night I could not sleep. I stared at the mess of mango branch and leaf shadows cast against my bedroom wall and ceiling by a bright full moon. Every minute or so, they swayed ever so slightly to the music of a breeze, an accompanying score to the scene resurfacing inside my head.

Click.

I was back in the bathroom with his penis in my hands.

No sooner had I pulled out my own putty penis from the trap opening of my American flag pajamas, faded from the many drip dryings under the tropic sun, that I began to push and pull on it, revising the scene in my head:

He slowly and steadily pushed my head down until I was eye to eye with it. It smelled sour, like a carton of milk that has sat in the refrigerator for a very long time.

"Kiss it. Taste it. Put it in your mouth," he whispered encouragingly.

I was flushed and frantic, flustered and fearful. My head throbbed as the velvet mushroom brushed my tongue.

I was no longer pushing and pulling but turning the head of my penis in a counterclockwise half turn, as if I was trying to open a bottle. I felt it harden. *It stood up! I never noticed it stand up before and with such force.* A surge came out of nowhere and ruptured at the tip of my penis. I panicked, held my breath for a second or two, and exhaled all the air I ever breathed in my life. I felt like passing out. But unlike the man, no arc of milk shot out of me. But it did not matter. I felt nothing as beautiful and wonderful and exciting and magical and fantastic as what I had felt that very moment. My first dry orgasm.

Within the routines of our household, I had established my own nocturnal ritual. After Mommy led us in prayer to have Jesus bless our family, especially Tatay and Lanelle, and to keep us safe and pure, she kissed us good night and turned off the lights. I waited until I could hear Jonas's sleeping breath before playing with myself. I did not always have to recreate the bathroom scene in my head. I simply looked down at my penis and willed it to respond. Either way, I could only fall asleep when the gushing sensation left my body.

I was once in the pantry attached to the clean kitchen. Although it was a school day, I must have been sick that morning and stayed home. It was dark except for a naked light bulb with a beaded metal cord by it that I could tug on and off. No one would know I was here playing with myself. I wanted to know if I could get the same sensation to happen during the day.

I sat on the cement floor. Its coldness seeped through my flannel pajama bottom. But that did not stop me from sweating as I stroked my penis for the longest time. I would feel the surge from within start up, then die down, then start up again. This was so much fun, I thought to myself. This way it did not have to end as quickly. Maybe I should do it during the day instead of at night. Could it work both day and night?

Pretty soon, the pantry was my secret hiding place. Collie would look for me throughout the house, shouting my name. Then she would run in a panic out the front door and into the street frantically yelling, "Jobert! Jobert!" Only then would I run back up to my bedroom and pretend to be asleep. Collie would return saying, "salamant Dios," in thankful prayer to God when she found me.

But one day...

"Jobert, what are you doing in there?"

I was so taken aback with Collie bursting into the pantry that my entire body jerked.

"What are you doing?" she said with a raised voice.

I had released my penis and stood up. She returned a quarter smile and put her hands on hips, staring down on me.

What was so funny?

I followed her stare down. My penis was somewhat hard and exposed, caught in the front flap of my pajamas. I turned around and shoved it in, then turned again and ran upstairs into my room, slamming and locking the door behind me. I was under the covers of my bed without a clue as to what to do or say.

When Mommy returned that evening, I ran up and reached to embrace her. She bent her knees to the floor and by the jerk in her neck, must have been surprised by the loud kiss I planted on her cheek. I cupped my hand against her left ear.

"Don't believe anything Collie tells you," I whispered.

"Jobert, get up."

"Whaaat?" I whined.

Rossana and Jonas came into focus as they looked out the window, their faces illuminated by bursts of fireworks—green and pink and orange. Pops and bangs echoed throughout the room, the windows trembling like the early morning porcelain plates shuttled across kitchens.

"Hurry, it's almost 1971," said Mommy.

We had fallen asleep in her room, as we had every day since the week before Christmas when she said we could. I thought it was because she missed Tatay and Lanelle. But part of me suspected she knew what I was up to at night and having me sleep on the fold-out beach chair next to her bed along with my brother and sister would severely limit the chances of my doing so.

Christmas had been quiet, at least compared to the year before, when both Tatay and Mommy had awakened all of us early on Christmas Day. We children had run down to the living room and looked under the silver tree. Like a hen, it had laid gifts that had not been there the day before. Red net stockings filled with chocolate coins in aluminum wrappers of red, gold, and silver hung next to the tree. Tatay read one of the labels for me. "Dear Jobert, Love Always From Santa."

This year, Mommy tried hard to make Christmas morning just as happy, but it was not the same. I even noticed that the label on the stocking filled with White Rabbit candy and Topsy Curls chocolate treats one could find at the corner sari-sari store was in her handwriting and read, "Dear Jobert, From Santa."

"Quick, over here. Hurry!" she said before starting her countdown from the number ten.

Mommy pushed the window open just as it struck midnight. The noise rushed inside, shaking through my bones and teeth as I stood alongside Rossana and Jonas, both screaming with glee. Mommy gave each of us a noisemaker to blow on, the kind that curls out like a frog's tongue before it squeals.

All of a sudden, firecrackers thundered through the hills. Our view of the city lights was blocked by black smoke within our own neighborhood with flashes, faster than lighting, bouncing back at us.

"Happy New Year!" Mommy said, squeezing all three of us as we tooted into the crazy night. "Happy New Year!" Happy New Year!" she repeated before sticking her neck out the window and blowing her own noisemaker. At that moment, for the first time since Tatay had left, Mommy laughed uncontrollably. She kept blowing and blowing but could not get hers to roll out its tongue or squeal. All she got was an airy emptiness. She kicked her head back still in laughter and wiped away a tear before kissing each of us.

"Happy New Year, Mommy," I said.

"Happy New Year, Job."

We must have locked eyes long enough to know we had no more to say. Mommy broke her stare and blew on the noisemaker once more. It worked this time.

"I'm glad the year is over," she said. "I'm glad your father will be returning home this year."

I, too, was glad that it was 1971. In three months I would turn seven. I wanted to say something sweet and smart. Something that would keep Mommy's smile in place, at least until Tatay and Lanelle finally returned home and we could be a whole, happy family again.

Lanelle showed up in June, back home first without Tatay. Something was different about her. She was taller and her hair longer, curlier than before. I was glad to see her, but it would take weeks, maybe months, for us to reacquaint ourselves. She said little of how life was in Connecticut. At fifteen, the curves on her chest were more defined than before she left, like Mommy and all women seemed to have. She also brought home two record albums, one called *Hair*, and the other by someone named Elton John. She played them over and over on the turntable. She dressed in bright shirts, as loud as her music, with rainbows bleeding in circular patterns.

But I wondered why Tatay was still not back when he said he would only be away for nine months. What would it be like to see him again? Would he have changed as Lanelle had?

Mommy picked up Tatay at the airport a month later, in late July. She insisted that we wait for him at home. When we saw him step out of the car, Rossana, Jonas, and I jumped on him, attacking him like eager puppies. He squatted down and hugged all three of us at once. Mommy shouted out to Collie and the others to carry in his suitcases. One was light blue and the other two were grey. They were Samsonite, as sturdy as tortoise shells, and their locks snapped open like TV antennae. And when Tatay opened each one in half, as if a casino clam, the crisp, clean scent of America exploded throughout the bedroom.

We sat on the bed as he took items out of the blue suitcase one by one, like bunnies out of a magician's hat. There were boxes of Nestlé Crunch, Butterfingers, and Pop Tarts along with Mary Quant makeup kits for Rossana and Lanelle and *Marvel* comic books for Jonas and me. It was like Christmas in July.

While we laid out all the goodies on the bed and sat by Tatay, Mommy fumbled through his briefcase, then she tore up a folder and papers she found in it and started to build a pile of Tatay's clothes from the other suitcases.

"Chica, let's take care of that later," he said.

She ignored him and his nickname for her.

"Chica, please!" he said in a louder voice. "We can discuss this matter later."

A shadow came over Mommy's face. What happened? Was not this supposed to be a happy moment now that we were all together again?

Mommy stormed out and headed straight for the dirty kitchen with Tatay's clothes in her arms. She acted as if Tatay never washed his clothes in America. I wondered how could all his clothes be dirty, even the ones still pinned to cardboard and wrapped in plastic?

I followed her while everyone else remained upstairs. She did not seem to care I was there watching her pour Tide detergent into the washing machine. She had not used it since the rainy season arrived, and handwashing was not possible outdoors.

"Take off those shorts and Jockeys too. Now," she said in a not so nice way. "Collie! Where are you?"

Mommy shoved Tatay's clothes inside the machine. She sighed twice, the second bigger than the first.

I panicked and ran upstairs, not wanting Collie to help me since she caught me playing with myself. I took off my shorts and briefs and put another set on, then ran back and handed the used ones to Mommy. I thought she was going to scream at any moment. She did not look at me as she threw my clothes in the wash. She slammed the machine's lid and walked out the side door of the kitchen. For the first time I was all by myself in the dirty kitchen. No yayas. No maids. No one.

Water started splashing in and underneath the closed flap. The washing machine gurgled and grinded like a monster awakening. I stretched my arms out to embrace its width. I shut my eyes and leaned my forehead on its metallic skin. It quivered against my chest and stomach as well as my crotch. And I was aroused. I sighed before walking out the side door and going inside the house through the clean kitchen, just as I assumed Mommy had.

When I emerged, there she was on bended knee, her arms stretched out, asking for a hug. And we did. She hugged me so tight, I must have lost a breath. I heard and felt her whimpers as I burrowed my head into her bosom. I would not soon forget that squeeze, like nothing wrong had ever happened and all was right between us. I would return to that snapshot for years to come, whenever she and I butted heads. But on that very day, at that very moment, I somehow knew I was her special one. No miracle was too grand to perform on my behalf. She would keep any secrets of mine close to her heart. And there was no need to ask about let alone understand what had transpired between her and Tatay.

2

Words Escape Me

ME

Me, me I am me
I think me is myself?
Me, I am myself, me, myself
Is me myself? Is there another me?
WHO AM I?

Author, ca. 1973

Antipolo/Quezon City, 1972

I thought Tatay had intuited my desire to express myself through writing when he handed me a tablet of blue-lined yellow paper. Or perhaps he wanted to ween me away from my TV addiction.

"Jot down whatever comes to mind," he said. "Don't worry about grammar."

After dinner, Tatay usually retreated to the family library in the basement and scribbled on his own pad of paper for hours without ever leaving his seat, long after the rest of us had gone to bed. He had just been elected as Secretary of the Constitutional Convention. He was going to help the Philippines govern itself better. More like a real democracy, he said. It sounded so important, Mommy warned us not to bother him and the only time we did so was to kiss him good night.

On his cluttered desk sat three silver cans that had had past lives as containers of evaporated milk from the supermarket. They seemed to grow tangerine pencils—a bouquet of lead tips Mommy kept sharp as needles. Tatay twirled them like bonsai batons between his thumb and index finger, pruning his thoughts over nationalism and better governance. He sighed every time he broke a tip or rubbed the tongue-pink eraser so vigorously that it tore through the page. I sometimes plucked out one or two of his pencils. I even chewed on the taffy-soft metallic band until the eraser would pop out and a bitter aftertaste would linger on my tongue.

"Where do you think pencils grow?" Mommy often yelled when she caught me in the act.

"Trees?" I replied in silence.

On most Sundays, right after Mass and lunch, Tatay asked, "have you something to show me?"

"Yes," I replied, eager to recite from my poetry collection written in the past week. I finished each poem with a pause, then stared up into his smudgy bifocals.

"That's excellent," he would say. I left, keen to call on my undefined muse for more poetry to flow out of me before the following Sunday.

At first I wrote about whatever caught my eye. Frogs. Coconuts. Grasshoppers. Bananas. Lizards on the ceiling. Matchbox cars. Then I tried writing of things swirling inside of me. When I was sad, rain poured on the page. When I was happy, the sun shone. When I felt loss, a balloon flew away. I was prolific, writing ten to twelve poems at a time.

If Tatay was my writing instructor, Mommy served as my literary agent. She mailed my poems to newspapers. My first ever published poem, "The Birds," was in the Sunday edition of *The Manila Chronicle*. I was designated a "Juvenile Gem" on August 20, 1972, a month before Ferdinand Marcos declared martial law when every newspaper, radio, and television station in the Philippines shut down. And in many ways, our life would be upended, causing us to wander far away, changing the trajectory of my upbringing to something more transnational if not transactional.

I must have known trouble loomed over the entire nation when the words flew from out of my left hand to perch on the electric blue wires cutting across the sunshine yellow of my paper and onto the printed page:

> The birds fly and fly everyday
> Birds will all of you stop?
> I keep seeing all of you fly
> Will all of you stop
> You never stop flying
> So pls. Stop

At recess, beyond the basketball court, through red dust mist, fourth graders kicked a soccer ball. It ricocheted against cleats and knee-high socks while navy blue shorts and white T-shirts pulled and shoved at one another, all falling to the ground like a heap of laundry. No one played by the rules, and judging by their loud laughter, no one seemed to care either.

We second graders were relegated to the grass playground, complete with a jungle gym, seesaws, and swings, which seemed more suitable for prep and first grade. Most of my class played tag with the school flagpole as home base. Dancing high above was the Philippine flag, full of symbolism we learned about in class. Its equal bands of patriotic crimson red and peaceful royal blue next to a white equilateral triangle at its hoist stood for liberty, equality, and fraternity. Within the triangle was a golden yellow sun of eight rays for the eight provinces. The sun itself represented freedom, unity, democracy, and sovereignty. There were also three stars for the three main island groups of Luzon, the Visayas, and Mindanao. It was a pretty flag to be proud of when compared to the fewer colors and simpler designs of neighboring Asian countries.

Tatay said we should be proud to be Filipino. Every time I looked up at the flag, I certainly was.

It was a month since Michael C_____, my best friend, had died. We used to throw paper airplanes at one another, eliciting giggles behind Miss Tomas's back as she demonstrated cursive loops and tails on the chalkboard. Together, he and I had cornered the market in coveted Snoopy and Woodstock stickers during recess, even fetching a whole PB&J. We divvied up our loot, cutting it diagonally into perfect halves. We were thick as thieves, hanging like bats on the monkey bars, each trying to hold on the longest, cackling as the blood rushed to our heads.

I had crumpled my face, asking our teacher, Miss Tomas, to repeat what she had told me. Michael couldn't be gone for good. The entire class climbed onto a bus, as if on a field trip, arriving at a church empty except for the sliver coffin. I tiptoed over to peer inside, but I was not tall enough. All I could see through the glass window was a ruffled wall of white satin.

I preferred sitting solo on the cement bench where Michael and I used to trade our stickers, where the green of the playground met the grey of the court. Dr. Seuss was resting on my crossed legs as I gazed longingly at the soccer field, like a kid too short to go on the best amusement park rides.

I wanted to be one of the fourth graders. They wore long khakis and black platform shoes as part of their uniform. The librarian shushed them as they giggled over pictures of topless Ifugao tribeswomen in *National Geographic.* They huddled at the far end of the cafeteria, trading secrets, speaking in code, as if plotting to rule the world. They were cool. They were untouchable. They were my idols.

It was a Friday in July, still early in the Filipino academic year, when I took my usual spot on the bench, and a dust cloud from the field blew across, headed right at me. I cupped my face. Just as I opened my eyes, a soccer ball came rolling up, resting just short of the grass line. It was soon eclipsed by a human shadow. I looked up and saw Chicklet teeth, a Cheshire Cat grin, a mop of black curls, and brown eyes big as Skippy peanut butter jar lids. I sat still as cartwheels spun inside of me.

"Sorry," he said.

"Ah, ah…it's okay, -kay," I said, embarrassed at my stutter. I never stuttered.

He knelt on his right knee, picked the ball up with both hands, looked up to see me staring back at him, then he turned around and ran back, the ball clutched in his left arm. I followed his every step all the way back into the soccer field. I glanced over my shoulder to see if anyone saw what had just happened. Everyone else was busy playing, leaving me to sigh and pretend the book I held was interesting.

The following Monday, I sat at the same spot and focused on him, again on the field. He shot two goals. I showed up religiously for three days straight. Then something odd started to happen. He appeared everywhere: in the cafeteria, in the library, in my notebook, and in my dreams. And just as our eyes would meet, I looked away, pretending not to care. I was cool. I acted casual. I was a boy. I was crushing inside.

The librarian jumped out from behind the circulation desk to hand me last year's yearbook. She didn't seem to suspect anything, just overly happy to be of assistance to my request. I walked to the corner table farthest away from anyone to fast flip through the pages, looking for the third grade section. I scanned the group pictures while keeping an eye on the library's entrance, fearful a classmate would enter and see me, wanting to know what was up. Then my index finger froze. There he was. Group Eight, third row, second from right. My breath was stuck in my stomach. He was smileless, though he looked straight into the camera. Right at me. He looked aloof. And handsome.

I matched the face to a name: Julius B _____.

I knew more about Julius B _____ than Julius B _____ knew I knew about him. He got me to lay out my crisp uniform of white buttoned short sleeve shirt and khaki shorts the night before and wake up early each school day. He had me brushing my teeth until my gums hurt. He got me to do my homework in the library and start playing soccer after school. I saw him in a Boy Scouts uniform on a Thursday, so I joined the Cub Scouts on a Friday. I started drinking Royal Tru-Orange and munching on Clover cheese chips just as he did at recess. When I was awarded Most Courteous in class for the first quarter, I quietly dedicated my certificate and ribbon to him.

Everything I did, I did for Julius. Never mind I was no one to him. Someday we would be something together, happy, without a care in the world. I no longer read during recess but still carried a book on me, a favorite being *The Five Chinese Brothers*, for fear that I would not have anything to shield me from my true motive of searching for Julius. I only wanted to be in his presence, no matter how distant.

I looked past the basketball court, beyond the soccer field, onto a grassy knoll. I daydreamed of Julius and me running up from opposite sides, meeting at the top of it. We were jumping up and down, as if on a trampoline, inhaling the pastel sky. We reached out to shake hands and embrace in midair. We were daredevil acrobats. Back on the ground, with arms stretched out, we leaned back against the warm, whistling breeze, strong enough to keep us from falling on our backs. We were laughing and shouting, our voices blowing into the valley below. The whole world was visible to us, but we were invisible to the entire universe.

"Jobert, how are classes going this week?"

Mrs. Santos sat with her legs crossed, her left knee sticking out from behind the metal desk and her leg swinging back and forth. On her thigh sat a notepad, where she seemed to scribble every word I had to say, even as I sat silent.

Right after Michael passed away, I spent a lot of time in Mrs. Santos's office. Every day for a week after my class said goodbye to Michael, I was called to meet with her during recess. Then it was cut back to every Tuesday, right after recess, during reading class. I looked forward to my time with her. She spoke to me like I was a fourth grader instead of a second grader. Always smiling, she asked lots of questions about school and home but never let me stop at a yes or no. Every answer had another question right behind it.

"And how does that make you feel?"

I thought she wanted to hear things were good. But if everything was good, she might have concluded all was back to normal for me. We would then have no reason to talk, and I would no longer visit her sky blue walled office with cotton ball clouds on the ceiling, a rainbow, a balloon like in *Around the World in 80 Days*, and air-conditioning.

"You like to read a lot don't you, Jobert?"

"Yes I do, Mrs. Santos"

"More than playing?"

"The same."

"Do you like playing tag?"

I looked at the clouds then down at my patent leather shoes. All her questions made me think of Michael. I wanted to tell Mrs. Santos that I still missed him. That would have made things easier for both of us. But Julius was constantly on my mind, buzzing like a bee trapped indoors, without an open window to escape through.

"How is the soccer club going?"

"Everything is fine, Mrs. Santos. Everything."

"Good," she said before flipping through the pages of her pad.

My thoughts must have strayed as the clouds began to move, blowing by and out of the room. Julius and I were back atop a grassy hill. We laid crown to crown and pointed at the white fluffy clouds we made out to be rabbits, old men with beards and dinosaurs, and cats and elephants. Birds flew by in V patterns.

"Mrs. Santos?"

"Yes, Jobert?"

"What does it mean when you think of someone all the time?"

"How so?" She uncrossed her legs and sat up straight.

"You see someone everywhere and you think about them all the time."

"Is this someone you used to know?"

"No."

"Is this person hurting you?"

"Uh, no *po*."

"Does it make you happy thinking of this person?"

I tilted my head from left to right. The clouds continued to fly by.

"Y-ye-yes. Yes it does." I did not want her to know it was a boy in school who made me happy.

"Well..." she said before balancing her ballpoint pen under her nose then putting it down. "You should write a story about this person," she concluded. "And don't worry about grammar."

With martial law declared and conflicting rumors of demonstrations and arrests bouncing all over the city like too many ping pong balls in play, classes were suspended for two weeks.

"I want to go to school today," I cried to Mommy.

"I'm sorry, you can't," she said, her eyes welling up.

Tatay had not come home when the convention disbanded. Marcos had had military units block Manila's main arteries, and a curfew was enforced from midnight to four in the morning. Lanelle said Tatay went into hiding because the authorities were after anyone who was anti-Marcos. Anyone who believed in a democracy was some endangered species, being hunted down by the military. My titos and titas would visit us and exchange stories in hushed tones on which family dynasties had the most to gain now that Marcos oversaw all infrastructure projects without any checks or balances. I also overheard First Lady Imelda Marcos was on a mission to be an A-list socialite on the global stage, spending government tax money to foster her ambitions. Regardless of whether relatives were with us or we were on our own, Mommy kept the front door double locked and warned us not to leave the house.

More than anything, we felt trapped. Mommy was worried sick over Tatay's whereabouts. We couldn't make any calls as the dial tone sputtered for days, and we'd heard rumors the telephones were tapped anyway. I wanted to run away and go back to school. I wanted recess. To play soccer. I wanted to see Julius.

With not much else to do at home, I decided I would write a book. I told Lanelle, and she offered to illustrate it. I wrote on my notepad about a boy named Julius who moved from Manila to Manhattan with his younger brother and parents. He missed all his friends back home, but he enjoyed his life in the new city, especially at Christmastime. He would make new friends and forget about all the old friends back home.

I finished my book in two days. Mommy edited my manuscript, and her ballpoint markings were everywhere, splotches of red all having to do with grammar.

"Do you like it, Mommy?"

"Who's Julius?"

"I made it up...like Orange Julius." I was relieved at my quick save, having just come back from the supermarket that had a stand selling the fruity drink, realizing I had to be more careful.

"Correct it, and it should be fine," she replied. I immediately did. Lanelle yanked it out of my hands and locked herself in her room for a day before presenting the book on a sketching pad.

"What do you think?" Lanelle asked Mommy as if I was not in the room.

"This is excellent," Mommy exclaimed.

"He looks like a girl," I said, raising my voice into a whine after seeing my hero's illustration.

"He does not," Lanelle barked back. She drew well, but Julius looked nothing like the real Julius. I felt helpless against both my literary agent and art director.

"We should show this to my publisher friend," Mommy said as she took the sketching pad away.

I ran into my room and sobbed into my pillow. No one understood. No one cared. I wanted to die but fell asleep instead. But not before I imagined Julius tumbling down the hill, disappearing into the valley below. I remained standing, rooted to the ground, barely able to utter his name into the howling wind.

"These are very colorful pictures," the publisher friend said over Catwoman glasses framed by her salt and pepper bun.

A week later, when it was deemed safe to drive around Manila with military forces at bay, Mommy made an appointment. She and I sat across from the woman at a long table made of tanguile wood with a map of the Philippines inlaid in mother of pearl. The woman's head moved along each page, mouthing my story.

"This is interesting," she said to Mommy. I stared at the largest island of Luzon partly hidden by a capiz coaster and a tall glass of Coke. I imagined the map turning into one of the entire world.

"But it is too American."

I looked up. She did not address me. She flipped through the sketching pad backward.

"It feels too familiar."

I had no idea what she meant.

Mommy nodded in agreement. "Jobert will try another story," she said before thanking her. I wiped off the sweat of Catwoman's clammy palm smeared all over my forehead.

Back at home, Mommy gave me a new tablet of lined paper.

"Why not write about a talking grasshopper?" she suggested.

I sat at my desk and stared at the blank page. I chewed on my pencil until it tasted of tree rot. I did not want to write about anything but Julius. That was the book I wanted to see come to life. A tear dripped onto the pad. Then another. And another until it was too soaked to hold any words. I rubbed my eyes, no longer knowing how to deal with thoughts of Julius mashing in my head and in my chest. It helped when I wrote about him, but no one liked my story. Mommy did but she, like Tatay, seemed to like everything I produced. I was afraid to show it to Mrs. Santos who would figure out in an instant who Julius was and would then tell my parents. Expressing my feelings and writing them down felt both right and dangerous. The mashing up inside was getting faster, pounding on my rib cage, crying to be set free.

Perhaps it was a force greater than Julius or myself. Whatever it was, it was certainly of *me*.

3

Beauty Scouts

Quezon City/Antipolo, 1973

Thoughts of Julius took up so much space inside my head, it hurt. I needed a distraction. I found one in the Cub Scouts where, after regular class time, I channeled my energies into the camaraderie and competitiveness of my troop, where I was prepared to be prepared. Where I first fully appreciated the calculus of risk and reward which fueled my newly acknowledged addiction for my parents' constant approval.

"Sir, how many patches are there in all?" I asked Mr. Santos, our Scout leader—no relation to Mrs. Santos the counselor. A much older man in his thirties, Mr. Santos crossed his noodle arms and rested his cleft chin on the palm of his hand while looking up at the buzzing ceiling fan, its stem vibrating, ready to propel downward and decapitate one or more of my fellow Scouts.

"That's a very good question, Jobert," he replied. "I'll get back to you on that."

However many there were, I wanted to collect every single one and display them on the shoulders, arms, and chest of my navy uniform like a decorated military general. Mommy stitched my patches so they would link up as a chain, certain, as I was, that many more would follow in my time at kawan or troop 674.

The first patch I earned was for handicrafts. I created a headband out of rainbow threads using a portable wooden loom. Every night for a week I wove and wove, even in front of the TV. Once I fell asleep while weaving and woke up the next morning to four more inches of cloth appearing out of nowhere. I never questioned how or why. It was Mommy's and my little conspiracy. When it came time to show off our finished product at the troop meeting, mine was eight inches longer than everyone else's.

I got desperate when the Fifth Annual Pet Jamboree came around. I didn't own anything to enter into any of the eighteen categories from the fastest feet and fiercest face to the sweetest smelling and cutest name, all promising trophies, certificates, and yes, patches. I had to have more patches than anyone else did. Every time I saw Mommy's smile and heard her hum as she pulled out the sewing kit, I knew it was the right goal to have. She, however, was not willing to invest in a dog, as money and mobility were foremost on her mind with Tatay's whereabouts still uncertain.

His presence seemed scant, as there was little mention of where he may be since martial law had been declared. I was oblivious to the roundup of Marcos's political enemies and the permanent disappearance of dissidents.

"Why not ask if someone will lend you a dog?" she suggested.

The only dogs I knew of were strays in and around Beverly Hills. I didn't think the judging panel would take too kindly to dogs with three legs and flies feasting on their gaping wounds. Mommy said, "pedigree counts," but I didn't know of any schools for dogs.

Our neighbors, the Bernardez family, owned caramel cocker spaniels I often played with. I promised them Perry, the largest and friendliest, would win a prize if they'd let me take him. But when he failed to do so, I cried all the way home. Did the judges not appreciate the moral anguish I endured in entering a dog that wasn't even mine? And that I had promised would be a winner? I crumpled up the flimsy certificate of participation I received and threw it away.

At the end-of-year evaluation in March, before school let out for the summer, members of the troop took turns conferencing with Mr. Santos outside the classroom in the hallway opening out into the playground. I was first up.

"Let's see...Jobert Abueva." He positioned a pen and ruler over his notebook, hunchbacked like a monk with a quill. "You've just received a patch for vegetable gardening and one for carpentry. By the way, that was quite a birdhouse you made. Three stories high."

"Thank you Mr. Santos." I beamed, discreetly rimming the newly sewn patch on my left sleeve with my finger.

"Hmm, you have eleven so far, three more than anyone else. How about taking a break this summer? Maybe you can help some of your friends with their projects. Are you enjoying the activities?"

I thought it was a trick question. I kept mute and nodded.

"Do you feel you're getting something out of each activity?"

"Yes, of course Mr. Santos...new skills." *Patches.*

"Good. I'll recommend you for honors at our next awards ceremony."

I liked the sound of that and thanked him even though it would be an entire summer and school quarter before the ceremony. I never quite understood why Cub Scouts did not coincide with the academic year. I thought of asking Mr. Santos but decided otherwise.

I stood up and, before entering the classroom, I turned to him and asked if he'd found out how many patches there were in total for one to acquire.

"I'll get back to you on that."

I entered third grade in June of 1973, and whatever crises lurked in the adult world could not pass through the school's tall metal gates crowned with barbed wire. In the morning, security guards in sheeny tight, dark blue uniforms opened all trunks and walked around with mirrors attached to the bottom of handles to check cars' underbellies, as if they were dentists looking for giant cavities. We had new teachers in third grade, but my troop remained intact, Mr. Santos included.

The biggest news in July was Margarita Moran winning the Miss Universe pageant held at the Coliseum by the Acropolis in Athens, Greece. It was broadcast live via satellite on a Sunday morning. For days after, it seemed to be the only thing all the adults talked about. Mr. Santos chatted excitedly with another male teacher his age as we filed into our troop meeting one afternoon. I tried to listen in on their furtive conversation and the way they stifled giggles as they brushed each other's arms when parting ways. Mr. Santos walked into the classroom with a grin.

"Hi, troop. Did you know Miss Philippines won Miss Universe?" he shouted, his arms rising up as if unto the heavens.

The entire troop leapt out of its seats, cheering jack-in-the-boxes. I was a half-beat behind everyone else not wanting to be the exception.

I would soon learn Filipinos took beauty contests very seriously, like the Venezuelans. Everyone looked forward to the annual *Binibining Pilipinas* competition, a beauty tournament with representatives to four different international pageants crowned in a single evening. TV shows were flooded with talk of pageants and declarations of the Philippines excelling on the world stage.

I had told Mommy and my aunts at a party how wonderful this was. They frowned at me as if I had said something sour that deserved a scolding, and they told me to run off and play with the other children.

With a clap of thunder, hundreds of hammers pounded the tin roof of our classroom, a curtain of water flowing onto the soccer field which became brown soup.

"Boys, I'll be right back." Mr. Santos stepped out of the classroom.

Paper airplanes glided past me while some boys played paper-rock-scissors. I stared out into the water world. I thought of Noah and his ark and all the animals he had to fit into it. *How did he choose which one should go?*

Mr. Santos returned. "I have an idea," he said.

He closed the door as we settled into our seats.

"Boys isn't it exciting that Miss Philippines won Miss Universe?"

We all nodded yes.

"Right. How about we reenact the Miss Universe beauty pageant?"

No one nodded.

What? Did I hear him right? A beauty pageant?

"I'll give you twenty minutes to make your costumes, and then we'll judge the winners." He left the room, closing the door behind him. *A beauty pageant?* Of the fourteen or so of us in the room, half went to work pulling out construction paper, scissors, and Elmer's glue from their desks. The other half returned to making paper airplanes.

I scoured the room. *What can I do different from everyone else?* After all, I was certain a patch was involved. *A patch for beauty? For acting? For Filipino Pride?* I ran to the closet in the corner of the room where the janitor kept cleaning supplies. I found a broomstick and a coconut husk used to shine the wooden platform at the front of the room by the blackboard. As I returned to my seat with these, other contestant wannabes caught on and ran over for what remained, shoving one another like shoppers at a flash sale in Shoemart.

"Okay, who's our first candidate?" asked Mr. Santos. He had brought in his teacher friend. The one he was making chismis with earlier to be the one and only judge.

A boy named Steve, with dark skin and a cereal bowl haircut, immediately stood up from behind me and sashayed towards the front with paper chains around his neck and waist.

"I am Miss Mexico," he said confidently in falsetto. The troop laughed. I was aghast. He twirled around and landed on one knee shouting, "Olé!" Mr. Santos led the applause.

"Good, good. Next...let's see, Francis."

Francis was *mestizo*, with Spanish blood. I always thought he was [Ameri]*cano* because of his light brown hair and milk white skin until we had a class on the origins of the Filipino people and how the Spaniard colonizers left their ethnic imprint. He didn't have Steve's grace or sissy air about him. He wore a green paper hat that fell like spiky leaves of a pineapple, and he had cut out a matching grass skirt.

"I am Miss Hawaii." His deep voice made me think of a tiki statue we had at home, not a hula dancer.

"Well, it's not a country but that's okay," chuckled Mr. Santos. The audience clapped as Francis found his spot on the platform next to Steve on the far right side by the locked door.

"Who wants to be next?" Mr. Santos scanned the room then pointed to someone named Peter.

Peter had taken the once white rag from the closet and wore it like a skirt. He had cut a big red circle and stuck it on his chest. He took baby geisha steps up to the platform.

"Miss Japan!" He bowed, but it was more like a curtsy. And he received a polite applause.

Mr. Santos looked at his watch and said we had time for one more.

"Who wants to go?" I raised my hand. "Okay, Jobert."

I took a deep breath and stood up with a Philippine flag I had drawn in art class taped to the broomstick in my left hand, balancing the coconut husk on my head. I tied my yellow kerchief, part of my troop uniform, into a sash. The room applauded like the rain outside as I made my way onto the stage. I walked naturally, neither sissy nor ape like.

"I am Miss Philippines," I declared. I received a standing ovation.

"Okay we have the results," Mr. Santos snapped as he took a folded piece of paper from his friend who smiled just a wee too much for what was going on.

The four of us on the platform stage moved to the center. All eyes were on us. A trickle of sweat crawled down my back. *What would Mommy say if she saw me like this?*

"The third runner up, is Miss Japan!" I stared out the window. Dark grey had now turned pitch black. The rain and applause were one and the same.

"The second runner up, is Miss Hawaii!" *Wait, why are we pretending to be girls?*

Steve closed the gap between himself and me and clasped my hand. The coconut husk nearly fell off my head.

"I will announce the first runner-up." Mr. Santos looked at us as if he had a script in his head. "Remember that if for any reason Miss Universe cannot fulfill her obligations, then the first runner-up becomes Miss Universe." The troop started a drum roll on their desktops. All I thought about was winning.

"The first runner-up....is Miss Mexico, Miss Philippines is Miss Universe!"

I feigned shock as Steve hugged and air kissed me before walking away, just as Miss USA did Margie Moran. Everyone leapt out of their seats, their cheers punctuated by lightning and thunder. *I won. I won.*

Mr. Santos asked me to parade around the room. By the time I sat down it was three thirty and time to go home. He asked us to put everything back where we found them and had us throw all our paper costumes into a trash bag by his desk.

"Let's keep this to ourselves. Only our troop, okay? Then we can do it again."

"Yes, Mr. Santos," we replied in unison.

"Scout's honor?"

"Scout's honor!"

Everyone was in a good mood as we headed to the waiting cars in the rain. I wondered how my troop mates reconciled their participation in the beauty pageant. I, myself, dreaded the drive home. There would be much traffic and flooding and Mommy would want to know everything about my day. I would tell her we covered current events at today's troop meeting. After all, Miss Universe was indeed news even though martial law was all around us, and we seemed to do whatever it took to escape, even if momentarily, from our reality. I was the last to leave as Mr. Santos was scribbling at his desk.

"Mr. Santos, do we get a patch for today's contest?"

He stared at me through his fogged-up glasses. "Not really."

"Why not?"

"Tell you what. Promise not to tell anyone about what happened at troop today, and I'll give you an extra patch."

"Okay...thank you, Mr. Santos." As I headed out the door I turned to him. "What will the patch be for?"

"I'll get back to you on that."

He never did. But I never pushed him either. Even when I did not receive any special honor at the awards ceremony, like Mr. Santos had promised, something deep down inside of me knew it was not worth protesting let alone telling Mommy about. What transpired that rainy day had to remain a secret, never to be repeated or mentioned about ever again. Scout's honor.

4

Novice at Heart

Kathmandu, 1974

A new adventure to the unknown awaited us after Mommy received Tatay's telegram for all of us to join him in Nepal. The idea appealed to me once I learned that it was not only home to Mt. Everest but Buddha's birthplace as well.

Despite a ban on international travel, weeks later in early April, we were somehow able to leave Manila to meet up with Tatay in Hong Kong. He then led us on a whirlwind India itinerary with each stop leaving an indelible impression: Calcutta (endless blocks of the homeless sleeping outdoors), New Delhi (snake charmer offering fat black boas around our necks for photos), Agra (luminescent under a full moon, the Taj Mahal built by Mughal Emperor Shah Jahan as a tomb for his favorite wife), Khajuraho (charcoal rubbings of *Kama Sutra* inspired sculptures), Varanasi (pyres emitting black smoke along the Ganges River), and our final destination, the Nepalese capital of Kathmandu.

I often found myself walking up the stairway to the roof of our new one-story cement home from which, on crisp mornings, I was lost in the horizon of the Himalayas jutting into the bluest of skies, omnipresent, enveloping the kingdom valley. The thrust of force it must have taken to form these topographical wonders was well beyond my comprehension. Yet I was fascinated and awestruck by the sheer beauty.

Sex symbols were very much in the open. Fertility shrines, with stone representations of the lingam (phallus) and yoni (vagina), adorned every street corner and household entranceway including our own. Women supposedly laid offerings of marigold petals and incense, especially during the waxing moon and when they were ready to get fertilized themselves. Once Tatay explained this, I stole a glance at the crude sculpture. A mix of impish and grotesque curiosity came over me every time I walked through our front door.

There was no television and only one radio station in Nepalese. We frequented the American Club, but that's just what they called it. Any foreign family could become a member. After the all-you-can-eat buffet, which left smiles on my parents whenever I returned for seconds and thirds on my own, they then dropped us kids at the theater room to watch the Saturday feature while they hung out at the bar and restaurant with other adults. We saw *Barbarella*, *Barefoot in the Park*, *Butch Cassidy and the Sundance Kid*—even *Soylent Green* and *Invasion of the Body Snatchers*. We wouldn't have been allowed to see these on our own elsewhere.

On other nights, before bed, we as a family took turns reading Bible passages that eventually took us through both the Old and New Testaments. We then would say the rosary. I soon came to understand how much my parents' faith meant to them and how they wanted us to become good Catholics even while living in a Hindu kingdom. They even managed to find an English Mass at St. Francis Xavier School about an hour from where we lived.

Tatay, having escaped uncertainty under Ferdinand Marcos's martial law, landed an assignment with the Ford Foundation and was lecturing at Tribhuvan, the Nepalese national university. On weekends, he took up painting under the tutelage of Chitrakar, a Nepalese master painter—although much later on I would learn that anyone named Chitrakar was an artist. Tatay's series of tantric images in electric acrylic colors penetrated me like a reverse Rorschach test.

While Lanelle attended a Nepalese arts college, Rossana, Jonas, and I were sent to British Primary School, a three-story house run by three English spinsters. It was a twenty minute walk up the hill from where we lived, and we were escorted every morning by Ram, our all-around household help, who on occasion would cook as well, until Mommy fired him on the spot after he was caught taking water directly from the faucet into the filtered water container before boiling it. That solved the mystery of why we all had the runs, especially Tatay.

My teacher was Miss Lycett. She was statuesque, with chestnut bangs curtaining her forehead, a long face with lines that cracked through her makeup. She taught four levels: Guppies, Sharks, Barracudas, and Whales, each group of no more than four with its own table and chairs, each with a distinct curriculum, all of us sardine-canned into the same room. During my year there, I started out a Shark and was upgraded halfway through to become a Whale, skipping Barracudas altogether.

My best friend, Stephen from Australia, was a fellow Whale. He had strawberry blonde hair and freckles that ran past his cheeks down to his neck. After school, he and I biked through the nearby hills and combined whatever rupees we had between the two of us to buy Indian chewing gum, which our parents warned us against, swearing it would make our teeth fall out. We equated this to going blind. We dared each other to masticate, wanting to see who first would lose a Chicklet tooth or start to have blurry vision.

Stephen lived next door to Katrine and Merethe U_____, Danish sisters who rounded out our Whale cluster. The four of us worked on the same math problems and a classroom mural of the scene from *The Iliad* when Ulysses blinded Cyclops.

Katrine was eleven, with shortish, dirty blond hair. She looked like the image on a Dutch Boy can of paint. Her brows were extra bushy, and her lips were curved into a permanent pout. She was pretty, but Merethe, at ten, was even prettier. She had lighter blond hair though it fell in waves down to her shoulders and blue eyes, blue like the pastel skies I smudged in all my drawings.

Our foursome's togetherness in the classroom carried over to the playground. We consciously segregated ourselves from the younger schools of fish. One August afternoon, Stephen and I were chasing a cow, considered holy by the Hindus, off the school premises while Katrine and Merethe each grabbed onto our shirttails. It was their tactic for getting close to the cow, but not too close. Merethe was weighing me down as I tried to shoo the cow out the gate entrance with a fallen tree branch. Just as I pushed her aside, she tripped, shirttail still in hand, bringing me down with her. Our tumble took on a life of its own, completing two full revolutions with me ending up on top of her.

"Jobert Abueva, over here, now!" Miss Lycett shouted as she waved her lanky arms furiously in the air, her body jerking as if a bug had crawled up her knickers.

Uh-oh. Merethe and I hastily stood up and brushed off grass and dirt clinging to our pants. We stood shoulder to shoulder, but then I took a step aside. Stephen and Katrine made faces at us behind Miss Lycett who then grabbed my wrists and dragged me up three flights into the classroom. I was playing out in my head a plausible explanation for what had just happened and why I should not be accused of anything untoward. There was to be no trial. Miss Lycett took the rubber slipper off her left foot and gave me four whacks on my buttocks.

She never saw the smirk on my face.

Later that afternoon, Stephen and I walked over to the girls' house and played hide and seek. Katrine was "it."

"...Eight, nine, ten. Here I come."

Merethe and I ran into the bedroom she and Katrine shared and hid inside their clothes closet. It was dark except for a crack at the bottom where daylight seeped in. We were squatting, with flowery smelling dresses on hangers above brushing our heads.

Our breaths slowed down as we waited for Katrine to find us. Then I detected the smell of talcum powder. I followed it to Merethe. Our shoulders touched. Without a word, we repositioned ourselves flush against one another. Our hands found each other and clasped. In an instant, I felt her lips glide across my nose, on the mole over my lip and finally, my mouth. Bull's-eye. She licked at my teeth.

My entire body twitched as if I had stuck my finger into an electric socket. I closed my eyes and stuck my tongue in her mouth, then grabbed her head and pressed my lips even tighter against hers. I wanted to swallow her entire head. We made smacking noises like rats gnawing on wood.

I lost track of time and space. The closet got stuffy, but I didn't care. My priority was our locked lips. But then a rattling sound followed by harsh light of day flooded over us. I could not tell which were bigger, Stephen's eyes or Katrine's mouth.

Stephen and Katrine soon began to mimic our every move. I would lie on top of Merethe, kissing her all over. Stephen would watch us, then walk over to Katrine's bed. In three days, they were managing just fine on their own.

I had woken up to the realization that I was this randy blob of molecules fueled by raging hormones. I had discovered girls and girl parts. And best of all, there was plenty of opportunity for hands-on application here in Kathmandu, which proved to be the perfect laboratory for my bubbling libido.

All four of us could not wait for school to end each day so we could resume our extracurricular activities. Miss Lycett often glanced, if not glared, at our table as we suppressed our giggles. She and I had frequent conversations with our eyes and necks:

"What's going on over there that's so funny?"

"Oh nothing. It doesn't involve you."

"Are you causing trouble? Do you want me to discipline you again?"

"Yes, please spank me, pretty please. Not really. You win, hag."

Every day after school I would return home for my bicycle. I told Mommy I was off to Stephen's. As long as I arrived back home before dusk and dinner was served, no questions were asked.

We swiftly headed for the girls' room. As their parents both worked, only the maid was in the house, talking to herself, overwhelmed by all her household chores. We simply locked the door and drew the curtains. Afternoon delight.

After we surveyed lips, earlobes, and breasts that did not yet exist, we progressed to thighs, knees, feet, and bottoms. Stephen and I would occasionally swap sisters, but this never lasted even fifteen minutes. Even then, I enjoyed watching them get it on and could not help, for a flitter, the thought of me in his arms instead of Katrine's. Having the two of us make out, albeit with sisters in separate beds, had appealed to me in a nebulous, twisted, curious sort of way.

Once, Merethe made a proposition that had me sweating and smiling all at once: "I'll show you mine if you show me yours." She unzipped her jeans and stretched open her panties, snapping them back so quickly, I couldn't see a thing except darkness between her legs. I still felt a surge run through me. I was erect.

Mommy asked why I was restless at dinner.

"Because I really like my school and my friends," I replied.

"Let's play hide and seek," was our code. And this went on for weeks. In October, on Merethe's birthday, I bought a ring from the jeweler which Mommy frequented on New Road, Kathmandu's commercial epicenter not far from Durbar Square where the virginal and prepubescent Kumari, or Living Goddess, resided. She was supposed to bring good luck if one saw her looking out from her tiny kind-of-prison window. But it was tough to do so whenever I walked by with the crowds that pushed and shoved to get a glimpse of the gem she represented. My interest was more toward a golden topaz. I told Tatay I wanted to give it to Merethe. He asked no questions and gladly handed me a wad of rupees. Merethe liked the ring and in return, loosened her panties, and showed me "hers" again.

One afternoon in November, Merethe suggested we take off all our clothes. I looked through her and felt my forehead as it grew warm and wet. I tried to crack a smile, but my mouth was sewn shut. As much as I had been the instigator all along, I was less certain about this next move. My stomach churned.

She took my hand and guided my fingers towards her pants. We had covered this territory before, but now my hand was trembling.

"What's wrong?" she asked.

"Oh nothing, just thinking."

Katrine and Stephen were necking, each with an eye on us. I closed my eyes and asked God not to be upset with me for what was about to happen. My head began to tremble. Then I heard a sucking sound.

"No!" Katrine screamed.

The maid was outside vacuuming around the window frame. Her eyes went big, bigger than the red dot bindi on her forehead, as she saw Stephen holding Katrine around the waist and probing her ear with his tongue. Merethe drew the curtain shut. None of us had realized it was only half drawn.

The girls were grounded the next day.

Two days later, Miss Lycett had a new cluster system. She had disbanded us Whales and split us into Mollusks (girls) and Plankton (boys). We had been relegated to the bottom of the food chain. Miss Lycett closely monitored playtime. Her constant gaze burned a hole in the nape of my neck.

Tatay announced the Ford Foundation was transferring him to Bangkok, Thailand, and we were leaving right after New Year's. Did this have anything to do with what had happened at the home of the U_____s?

My last afternoon at British Primary School was the Christmas pageant held at the British Council auditorium. I played the angel announcing to the shepherds and the rapt audience, "For unto you is born this day in the city of David a savior, who is Christ the Lord." As I enunciated every syllable from the book of Luke, I could not help but think that, given my lusty mindset, I was anything but a heavenly messenger of good news.

As we concluded the program with a *Silent Night-Joy to The World* sing-a-long and headed backstage and onto a side entrance where our parents were to meet us, Stephen and I caught up with Katrine and Merethe. They did not seem to have the spirit of the season on their blank faces.

"Come visit me in Thailand," I said.

"Okay," Katrine replied.

Merethe looked at me with hurt eyes.

"Bye, Merethe. I will miss you."

She remained silent and looked up then down on the cement flooring. "Bye Jobert. I really like to…"

A blue-grey Renault, which looked like a poor cousin of the Love Bug, honked incessantly as it stopped right in front of us.

"Katrine, Merethe. In the car now!" their mother commanded.

Merethe ran up to her. "Mummy, can we see Jobert off at the airport?"

Her mother looked at me then at Merethe. "No, we can't. I have work."

"But he's leaving on Saturday."

"I said I have work." Her tone was terse. Mrs. U_____ stretched her neck out of the window. "Jobert, good luck. Be good."

Katrine waved goodbye while Merethe looked out the car's rear window with no hint of what she was feeling. Stephen stood back as I took a step forward. I wanted to run alongside the car, waving and shouting until it was too fast for me, like in those American movies, but my feet were glued to the ground. I stood helpless, wanting to know what Merethe was about to tell me.

The car took a right at the guarded entrance, raising a cloud of dust from the graveled road. I turned to Stephen, my eyes wet and chest heavy. I wanted to disintegrate into dust myself. It seemed to be the best possible outcome at that very moment.

He came up to me and put his hand on my shoulder. I turned, and we hugged hard.

"By the way," he said, "Merethe wanted me to give you this." He opened his palm to reveal the ring I had given her. I blinked. *Why did she not keep it?* I then grabbed it and clenched it in my fist. Stephen said goodbye and walked toward his parents who were waiting for him among the line of cars. And as he too was no longer in sight, I swore never to do all the things Merethe and I did with another girl ever again. I then tossed the ring into a nearby trash can, then sat on a bench, head down, palms to my eyes, waiting for my parents to pick me up.

5

Under My Umbrella

Bangkok, 1975

The city of angels, the great city, the eternal jewel city, the impregnable city of God Indra, the grand capital of the world endowed with nine precious gems, the happy city, abounding in an enormous Royal Palace that resembles the heavenly abode where reigns the reincarnated god, a city given by Indra and built by Vishnukarma – translation of the official name for the Thai capital, Khrung Thep, making it the longest recorded name in the world as entered in the Guinness Book of World Records.

November's monsoon rains showed no mercy on this City of Angels known as Bangkok to foreigners or farangs in local lingo. The constant drumbeat turned to white noise we endured through our sleep and most of our waking hours. Muddy water had started seeping into the school bus as if it was at the famed floating market. You couldn't tell what were side street sois and what was canal khlongs, a system that webbed throughout this so-called Venice of the East.

Classes were soon cancelled at Ruam Rudee International School for nearly three weeks. We were back to a Catholic-based curriculum. Instead of Jesuits in Manila, it was the Redemptorists. Tatay and Mommy were still pleased we were receiving a proper parochial education after nearly a year of British secular instruction. We also attended Sunday Mass on its premises, at Holy Redeemer Church, a tall white wat or temple inspired concrete structure, complete with gold, red, and green tiled flourishes on its rooftop, which wing tipped into the sky like the graceful, lively hands of a traditional Thai dancer. We learned to wai with our prayer-pressed hands and slight bows as we offered our "peace be with you" to other parishioners. But with so much rain, we forwent Mass and instead said the rosary at home.

Still, monks in saffron robes waded shin-deep through the neighborhood, and our household staff anticipated their early morning arrival at the front gate to tak bat by offering alms of cooked rice for their bowls.

From my bedroom window, I spied Khun Shalo, our housekeeper, a young, slim, pony-tailed woman in her twenties, wearing a long silk wrap down to her ankles. Instead of rushing us ready for school, every day she left a small bowl of rice and a cup of neon red strawberry-flavored Fanta in a cup in the spirit house that stood diagonally atop a concrete pillar pedestal in a corner of our backyard, shaded by a teak tree and curtained by a bamboo grove. The spirit house resembled the Royal Palace made of intricate glass tiles, glinting when there was morning sunlight. I tried to spot these mini shrines everywhere I went, with their abundance of offerings that induced the sweet-toothed spirits into protecting the houses and buildings.

Khun Shalo, along with Khun Surat, our cook, and her husband, Khun Shaman, who had an unknown day job but was a super handyman around the property, lived in satellite quarters and a 'dirty kitchen' connected by an outdoor roofed walkway to the main house, two stories of glass and hardwood which the Ford Foundation rented for us from a Thai general and whose domestic staff was at our service.

We were introduced to tangy thom kha gai and burning-mouth green, yellow, and red coconut curries as well as hot bowls of glass noodles with chili and lemongrass and lime as an after-school treat. Pad thai became my boyhood spaghetti and meatballs. And when the November full moon approached, they taught us how to weave boats out of banana stalks and leaves we then filled with marigold petals, a candle, incense sticks, and a few baht coins. We would release our creations into a nearby khlong after making a wish along with thousands of others throughout the kingdom, as part of the Loi Krathong festival in honor of the river spirits that lived alongside humans.

For that one night, the rain gave way to a cameo appearance by the full moon itself. And like the mystical glow of a thousand points of oil-wicked lamp lights that dotted all of Kathmandu during Diwali, now handprinted on my heart, so too was the tranquil trance of a krathong flotilla. It left me in a moment of awe and wonderment, planting seeds of spirituality that would fertilize and eventually sprout during my adulthood.

Rossana, Jonas and I gawked at flowery fireworks above and rowdily reached for baskets floated from farther up the khlong, still fragrant though their candles were out, to pocket baht coins. This was much to the bemusement of Khun Shalo.

Despite all the revelry, I sorely missed going to school and had made it my water wish that we return soon. I missed Mrs. Sloan's mixed grade accelerated 4-5-6 class which I transferred into after a few months in Mrs. Wongpakdee's fifth grade class and bypassing regular sixth grade. I even missed the odd instance when Mr. M_____, a substitute teacher and John Denver lookalike with a beard, would rock back and forth behind me, his soft, warm crotch brushing the back of my head as we sat at a low, round table in the library working on our social studies project. I had picked out Saskatchewan from a bowl filled with Canadian provinces and Australian states and received an A+ for having the gumption to borrow a film reel from the Canadian Embassy that showed forty minutes of Saskatoon's harsh winters. We saw lots of howling wind and snowdrifts that no one in these Southeast Asian tropics was able to relate to.

I missed our Filipina music teacher whose name I could no longer recall. She had her pulse on the hits of the day, leading us in song as she strummed her guitar to *Country Roads, Laughter in the Rain, I Write the Songs,* and *Top of the World. Kookaburra* may have been the exception, but it was a favorite as the entire class belted out at the top of our lungs trying not to get off track from the round we were assigned to, boys entering a stanza after girls, and finishing up with the last line together.

What I missed most was being around my two closest friends, Robert and Piyun. Robert was from Sweden, and his blinding blond hair and chiseled jaws made me dart glances at him in class every chance I got. I did the same with Piyun from Laos. Her face was mooncake round and pastry white, with big black dot eyes and a sweet smile. At lunchtime, I would position myself to sit alongside one of them. I believed God actually answered prayers when I got both of them to sit one either side of me one day. After knowing what had been possible with Stephen, Merethe, and Katrine back in Kathmandu, I wondered whether the same could happen with the three of us: Robert, Piyun, and me.

"Mommy, may I have a birthday party?"

"Your birthday's not 'til March," she said, creases over her brows.

"We just started school then so I didn't have any friends on my birthday. Now we're leaving after Christmas again. I want to have a goodbye party."

"Ah. Okay. Okay. How many are in your class?"

"No, no. I want to invite my friends only."

"Okay, who then? How many?"

"Robert and Piyun."

"Just the two of them?"

"And no one else!"

As soon as December arrived, clear skies returned as did the sun's scorch, and flood waters began to subside. We were back in school getting ready for the Christmas talent show and our class was practicing a medley of *Jingle Bells*, *Walking in a Winter Wonderland*, and *We Wish You a Merry Christmas*. Tatay had announced we were moving again, this time back home to the Philippines.

I lamented that it was unfair to uproot us yet again and to abandon our friends. I milked the situation and got my parents to agree to my hosting a belated birthday/Christmas/farewell/(I love Robert and Piyun) party.

"Are you both free on Saturday?" I asked, breathless from playing patintero at recess. Patintero was a Filipino game of tagging members on the opposing team trying to score by running the gauntlet one rectangle at a time and back. The game was already popular at Ruam Rudee even before I showed up, since the student body had quite a few Filipinos.

To Robert's and Piyun's enthusiastic yesses, I opened up my flip-top desk back in class and presented them with invitations I had created the night before using pastels to depict sun and surf and stick figures of the three of us. Mommy had me add our home address and telephone number so she and their parents could make proper arrangements for our driver to fetch them.

I had four days to prepare for my party. I giddily painted a watercolor of a donkey separated from its tail, which I would then cut out. I took a chair out of Tatay's home office and looked through his collection of records, picking out his worn-out Vikki Carr album to use for a game of musical chairs. I asked for a clay pot that I could fill with candy then hoist up as a Filipino pukpok palayo version of a piñata. I even asked Khun Shalo to help me weave banana leaf baskets for my guests to collect their winnings. Without my asking her to do so, Mommy requested Khun Surat to bake a cake.

I woke up to rolling thunder at six a.m. on the day of my party. Upon looking out into the dark overcast, I made a quick sign of the cross then turned to the spirit house below and bowed with pinched eyes, begging for it not to rain. A few minutes later, with a flash of lightning and a clap of thunder, a waterfall from the rooftop blurred out the entire backyard.

"It looks bad," said Mommy. "We may have to cancel."

It was close to noon. "But the driver is here. He made it here. Right?"

"He said that it's starting to flood by Democracy Monument."

Democracy Monument was the roundabout in the center of the city on Ratchadamnoen Avenue, the main artery Robert and Piyun would have to be driven through to get to where I lived.

"Call their parents. Please?" It was a command and a beg.

I ran back to my room and prayed even harder, incanting. My wai turned into a crumple of white knuckles as Mommy made phone calls from downstairs. I telegraphed mind messages, first to Robert, then to Piyun, to please come to my party. *Please. Please. Please.*

It was past three thirty in the afternoon when they showed up at my front door an hour and a half late. I wanted to hug them both at once but instead blurted out, "Welcome!"

The rain had eased up. Mommy must have negotiated and given the all clear for my guests to be fetched and delivered. It felt like receiving the best Christmas gifts one could ever ask for. Like a broken record, Mommy repeatedly told me my party was to last no more than two hours. It had to end before nightfall so she could see the children home safely.

Robert sported a fresh haircut, short on the sides and kissably cute. He wore a white collared shirt, a light blue jacket, charcoal grey trousers, and cordovan leather shoes. Piyun was in a long, white lace dress with a Virgin Mary blue ribbon belt as if she was ready to receive her first holy communion. Or get married. Her short socks matched her dress, as did her white leather sandals. She too was smoochable.

We sat in the living room as Tatay and Mommy initiated a line of questioning. What do your parents do? Are you in Catechism class as well? What would you like to be when you grow up?

I interrupted the interrogation. "Let's eat!"

The table had already been set. I pulled out chairs for Piyun to my left, Robert to my right, and me at the head of the table, all of us at points of an equilateral triangle. My family took a hint as I exaggerate-smiled at them until they fully retreated upstairs and left us to our late lunch of steamed rice, pad thai, green papaya salad, and massaman curry.

I didn't say anything about it not being my birthday, but I did divulge the fact that my family was moving away after Christmas.

"Oh, okay" they said in unison, turning their heads toward me then right back at their own plates to eat in silence. My matter-of-fact delivery was met with a reflexive response of unmoved utterance. I got it. We had all become blasé to our reality. We were expat children who had been somewhere else and were bound to be elsewhere before we even knew it.

We were what would be called "Third Culture Kids" (or TCKs), who spend our formative years in places that are not our parents' homeland. Our identities rooted in people rather than places, our little lives constantly disrupted, learning to live in the moment including second helpings of pad thai as well as second pours of condensed milk sweetened iced tea.

We talked about topics that preoccupied us: Thai tamarind candy that made our bellies ache, the screening of Bruce Lee's *Enter the Dragon* we had all seen at the school gymnasium on movie night, the nun who clapped her hands in the hallway telling us to stop running, a rundown of all our teachers and classmates—who we liked and disliked without much reason why. We chortled until Mommy reappeared to say that Robert and Piyun had to leave soon as it had started to drizzle. She asked Khun Surat to bring out the white cake. It had a blue and red krathong boat design and read "Sawasdee," the all-purpose Thai greeting for hello and farewell.

"Can they bring their cake home instead? We haven't even played any games," I said.

She motioned for the cake to be taken away and asked Khun Surat to have the driver get ready.

"Let's go!"

I prompted Robert and Piyun to follow me through the living room and out onto a brick tiled outdoor dining space which faced the backyard. The donkey poster was taped against one of the sliding glass doors and the palayo was hoisted yea high above. A tree branch which Khun Shaman had hand-shaved smooth stood waiting to be used as the whacker to the pot.

But then came the not-so-distant rumbling of a bowling ball thrown onto its alley in the sky. And fat warm drops were now landing on our faces.

"Stay here. Don't move," I said.

"No!" Piyun shouted then began to laugh.

"Yes!" Robert responded just as loud, and he too laughed.

"Be right back!"

I ran into the vestibule and grabbed the largest umbrella I could find. It was red and gold, handcrafted out of waxed paper and bamboo, native to Chiang Mai in the north. As I opened it for Robert, Piyun, and I to get under, a flash of lightning and thunder clapped right above us, this time a ten-pin strike. We all shrieked.

I looked into Piyun's eyes and then Robert's. We scrunched under the umbrella, futilely trying to stay dry. And as if on cue, it began to pour, the deafening kind of rain, and we all laughed, even snorted, knocking our heads back, getting our clothes soaked in the deluge. I knew that this was as good as it was ever going to get; that the three of us would never be this close ever again.

6

Boat People in the Basement

Antipolo, 1976

We left Bangkok at the tail end of 1975 and landed in Manila an hour after New Year's. The firefly lights in the distance were fireworks along Manila Bay and all across the sprawling metropolis. I saw the reflection of my smile on the KLM 747's window. So what if there was a curfew each night under martial law except perhaps this very night? Or that leaving the country ever again would be near impossible under even tighter travel sanctions? And that Marcos and his cronies were growing fat with greed and graft, crime and corruption, the poverty line continually rising and drowning the masses.

After two years abroad, it was good to be back home and reacquaint ourselves with neighborhood kids and go on long bike rides to the edge of our subdivision. To fix up my bedroom desk with books and supplies as a sort of home office, long before I was aware of its concept. To get back to a bookmarked page of *The Hardy Boys* I had stopped reading long ago, the plot and its characters in a haze.

As soon as the van that met us at the airport parked at No. 6 Dahlia Drive, Beverly Hills Subdivision, Antipolo, Rizal, Philippines, Rossana, Jonas and I ran through the living and dining rooms, into both the clean and dirty kitchens, and up to all four bedrooms and out into the balcony. We nearly tore down the screen of a side door that led down to the cabaña with the barbecue pit as well as the family library that also served as Tatay's office where I had once come across issues of *Playboy* and *Hustler* underneath piles of *House and Garden*. We were out of breath but full of laughs. The geography of home required no maps. We could pick up right where we had left off.

As for school, I did not want to return to an all-boys parochial after discovering co-ed education. Lucky for me, Ateneo was already three-quarters through its academic year. Somehow, my siblings jumped right back into the

Philippine school system, whereas I ended up at International School where I did not have to wear uniforms, and I got to enjoy air-conditioned classrooms with the children of Manila's expats and echelons of Filipino society.

I made quick friends with Lars from Stockholm who in turn introduced me to other Swedish classmates with whom I got to attend parties at their homes and dance to ABBA, and I liked being the only non-Swede in attendance. I once had a date with a Filipina girl named Gina. We held hands throughout all of *Rocky*. It seemed to be the thing to do. Without any sparks and a numb, clammy palm as the credits rolled, that was the extent of that.

My family quickly settled into our own routines. I left home with Tatay before the sun was awake to avoid snail traffic into Makati, the financial district where both my school and Tatay's office were located. Lanelle drove Rossana and Jonas to Maryknoll and U.P. (University of the Philippines) respectively. She herself continued to study fine arts at U.P. We all then met up for dinner as the sun got sleepy, yawning colors across the long horizon from Laguna de Bay and Metro Manila through to next door Quezon City and the silhouette of Mount Arayat all the way out in Pampanga province. Mommy stayed home, got the house back in order, and trained a new household brigade that, like before we left, included a maid, lavendera, and a gardener but only one yaya.

On weekends after dinner, we sat out on the porch Tatay had added when he had the house rebuilt after typhoon Yoling destroyed it back in 1972. It was rebuilt with five times the amount of concrete. The third floor lookout had a metal railing that ran the length of the house and connected all our bedrooms, each with its own entrance. We often chatted about the week past, counted the stars, told ghost stories, and played Cluedo or Monopoly.

One April night after my twelfth birthday, as Mommy served chicken adobo, rice, and green leaf pechay, Tatay said we would have houseguests for two or three months. *Two or three months? This was unheard of.* Tatay's youngest brother, Tito Tony, stayed with us for nearly a month at one point because he spent his rent money on "Gone with the Wind" memorabilia and scrapbooks of his favorite Filipino actresses, Susan Roces and Amelia Fuentes. What awful thing could these guests-to-be have committed to warrant such an extended stay?

"Dr. Giao is a friend who taught psychology at the University of Saigon," he said. "He was a visiting professor at U.P. That's how I know him."

I dropped the chicken drumstick onto my plate. *Saigon? Vietnam!*

"He called last week from Palawan. He arrived two weeks ago with his wife and two daughters." I focused in on Tatay's mouth as he spoke. I was aware of the influx of Vietnamese arriving by boat, overwhelming the refugee camps and towns as they landed on the shores of Palawan, south of Manila. Photo images of tearful farewells amidst the exodus and that of naked children crying, running away from exploding napalm in *Life* magazine remained plastered in my head. Mommy had once mentioned when we drove by the seedy side streets of Pat Pong in Bangkok that swarms of out-of-uniform soldiers we passed by were on R&R from the war. I did not understand about a war that killed many Americans and that families ran to greet their fathers on tarmacs upon their return to the United States. What I did know was that anyone escaping by boat had no intention of returning.

"Tatay, how did they get here?" I asked, already sure of his answer.

"They were on a boat for ten days." *Oh my God, real live boat people.* I was alarmed and enthralled all at once. Everyone spoke of their plight, but now they were going to live with us under the same roof, in our happy home.

"Where are they going to stay?" Lanelle asked. *Yes, where are they going to stay?* Our guest room was still packed with unopened boxes shipped from Bangkok. Even if we cleared them all out, it could not fit a family of four. I didn't want to move out of my room which my brother and I shared. *Did the boat people sleep like us anyway?*

"We'll set up cots in the library in the basement," said Mommy.

"Did they lose everything?" I asked.

"I'm afraid so," Tatay replied. "I heard they are on the waitlist to go to the States." *The United States? Wow.* They escaped on a boat, survived for ten days on the South China Sea, landed on Palawan, and were now on their way to America via us here in Antipolo. I had yet to meet them, though I was already envious. I loved my home, but I too wondered whether things would continue to deteriorate in the Philippines as I would hear my parents and their friends say. Perhaps we all had to have an escape plan.

"When will they show up? When? When?" My incessant interrogation.

"What's today? Monday? This coming Friday." he replied.

That was in four days. Hardly any time to prepare, even though I wasn't quite sure what I needed to do. But it was too soon for a disruption of this magnitude in my mind. I was eager and nervous about boat people in the basement. They must have had incredible stories to tell.

My investigator interview was lined up. *What was it like to be out in the open sea? Did you know where you were headed? How many of you were onboard? What did you eat to survive?* So many questions flooded into my head. Perhaps they could reenact their adventure. Even better, they could tell their tale to my neighbors who would line up at the ticket booth I imagined setting up in our garage.

"Mommy, can we prepare them a welcome dinner?"

This time, Tatay, Mommy, and Lanelle guffawed. "Of course we can," she answered. "We'll make sure they enjoy a good Filipino dinner and genuine Filipino hospitality." I twisted within with more questions. *What if they really like it here and live in my very own house?*

Dr. and Mrs. Giao, and their daughters, Lo-an and Nguyen, looked lost and bewildered as we escorted them downstairs to the library. I had helped Mommy make space on the bookshelves and bring down foldout beds from camping trips past, as well as bedsheets and towels.

My hands were clammy, and my smile hurt as I stole stares at Lo-an and Nguyen, both quiet and avoiding eye contact as we started a dinner the likes of which I had not seen prepared before. It was more festive than a Noche Buena after Christmas Midnight Mass: kare-kare oxtail soup in peanut sauce, glass noodle pancit, tangy tamarind stew sinigang with chunks of milkfish and strands of pechay, as well as lots of chicken adobo. The adults clinked their mugs of the bitter San Miguel beer and seemed to speak in code and at times whispers on their half of the table. Something about 'atrocities.'

I was itching to say something to Lo-an, who was about my age and sat right next to me. Nguyen, who was fifteen, sat next to Lanelle. They cracked a smile now and then but hardly had a sustained conversation. Lanelle asked if they liked music and had heard of Stevie Wonder. Nguyen, in broken English, also spoke of Janis Ian and Captain & Tennille. The ice had broken. Our Asian cultural divide had been united by our mutual admiration for American pop music. And from there on out, their English vocabulary seemed to expand like a balloon filling up with helium out of a language tank.

Mrs. Giao and her daughters dressed in áo dài: the traditional Vietnamese garb of flared pants and an extra-long see-through blouse with floral prints reaching down to their shins, slits coming all the way up to their hips on either side to the point that you could see skin. It looked cool and sexy. They all sported similar hairstyles—long and straight and silky like the shampoo ads on TV. Their skins were smooth, almost porcelain glossy.

By the time Mommy brought out a leche flan and Magnolia brand purple yam ube ice cream, there was so much laughter going around even faster than the Lazy Susan being spun for seconds and thirds.

As the days turned to weeks and into a month, I thought Mommy would be concerned about having to feed and manage a barrio or barangay full of bodies—fourteen in all including the household help. But she seemed genuinely happy to have the company during the day. Before long, she, Mrs. Giao, and her girls seemed quite chatty, though more so with their hands as they did not always seem to understand one another.

A new routine had taken hold. Dr. Giao accompanied Tatay to the Ford Foundation after dropping me at school during the week while Mrs. Giao, Lo-an, and Nguyen stayed home to help Mommy prepare dinner starting with morning motor tricycle trips into Antipolo proper to shop at the open wet market.

We soon alternated between Filipino and Vietnamese dinners. I could not wait to get home to try the strange, sweet, sour, salty sauces drenched over popcorn shrimp. My other favorite was the Vietnamese version of uncooked translucent tortilla-like lumpia spring rolls called gỏi cuốn, filled with pork, prawn, lemongrass, and bean sprouts. Even the Filipino meals I was accustomed to started to taste better than usual. And there were always way too many leftovers.

For the next three months, our happy home had become very active. Lo-an and Nguyen taught us to count from one to ten in Vietnamese and we would return the favor in Filipino, Thai, and Nepali. Although my parents installed a small TV in the library, Lanelle often invited the girls upstairs to watch the less staticky, sharper-colored TV with us. We played Scrabble and Monopoly but never seemed to keep score properly let alone finish a game. We were just happy to be around one another.

Once, when we were alone watching TV, I asked Lo-an to tell me how they had escaped Vietnam. She jerked her head and let out an audible sigh. *Oh no, maybe I had upset her.* She looked down on the tile floor, stood up to turn off the TV, then took another breath and began her story. All I could recall were her very first words: "It rained bombs everywhere."

I egged Lo-an at every possible opportunity to tell me more about the war but only when we were alone. Whenever she described a bloodied baby or a girl's body thrown overboard, I cringed and exaggerated covering my ears. She talked of her parents paying their way out with jewelry and of the beautiful home with the lush tropical garden they had abandoned. When I asked her to describe her bedroom, she started to sob. All I could do was hold back my own tears. I wanted to tender touch her shoulder but held back.

I finally managed to string together her story. *Apocalypse Now* had just started shooting scenes on Clark Air Base and U.S. Naval Base Subic Bay not far from Olongapo, a notorious nocturnal hangout for off-duty soldiers and sailors. I understood it to be a wild, titillating scene of sex and booze and babies of mixed race. I even recalled my parents welcoming a retired American airman to stay with us for a few weeks. I had found him ruggedly handsome and tried to be around him as much as possible without being suspicious. He said he was an advisor on the movie, flying helicopters, but I could already roll the movie in my mind of what Lo-an and her family had lived through.

It left me scared and sick. At times I would dream, even in my siesta, of girls and boys my age protecting their faces from the briny ocean sun. I began to cry for Mommy as people were falling off the boat and disappearing into the murkiness below. I saw our happy home in the distance, floating away until it too was swallowed by an angry sea.

In mid-July, we had our last Vietnamese meal before the Giaos were to fly to San Francisco. Dr. Giao's fellowship at Oakland State University had come through. Their multiple visits to the American Embassy in Manila ended with entry visas granted and stamped on their passports. I pretended I had a stamp on my passport too, and I could leave for America forever along with them.

The week before, we'd all watched the U.S. bicentennial celebrations on TV. Fireworks on the New York harbor and along the promenade in Washington, D.C. did not seem to fit on the screen. Lo-an's and Nguyen's eyes bulged as they gasped and giggled, clasping each other's wrists with both hands and whispering something in Vietnamese. While I was genuinely happy that they were headed to America, I, was envious as well.

We loaded the van that would take them to Manila International Airport with the new suitcases they had purchased at Shoemart, and everyone exchanged hugs and 'all the bests' and 'good lucks.'

Lo-an turned to me. "Jobert, thank you for listening."

"Thank you for telling," I said. We hugged.

Tatay, Mommy, Lanelle, Rossana, Jonas, and I stood together as if we were posing for a photo, waving as the van drove down the end of Dahlia Drive, many arms waving back out of its windows.

I did not know then how the Giao family's American story would unfold: Lo-an would become a pediatrician after graduating from UC Berkley and Stanford, and Nguyen, after studying engineering at Stanford, would work at NASA.

Nor did I know then that in a few years, I would write a poem and enter it in a speech competition, get it published in *Poetry Nippon*, and recite it at a refugee symposium in Tokyo not fully appreciating how I was inspired by the Giao girls, not realizing it would remain someone's story even to this day.

Boat Girl

Her name is Ning Lam and she's on a boat
With a hundred others it can hardly float

Her family and friends left home weeks ago
To run away from the dreaded foe

All their possessions they left behind
Freedom and security they hope to find

Food is scarce, tasteless, uncooked
Fish and seaweed simply unhooked

Disease spreads victimizing the weak
Half of them die the rest are left meek

The vast sea could be calm and kind
But will her merciless fury unwind?

Ning Lam's father holds the compass in hand
His goal to bring everyone upon dry sand

From country to country they try to land
No government willing to give a hand

Back at sea they despair
For land no one will share

As the perilous journey will not cease
Emaciated, they slowly decrease

Her sister died some days ago
The body with many others is in the depths below

Yet, as she looks ahead there lurk dangers
For they must face many more strangers

Pirates come to rob and abuse
The few sickly women and what's left to use

Her mother is taken away, Ning Lam knows as she hides
Her father fights and is tossed into the tides

No compass in hand
No sight of dry sand

Her only companion is dying
She is left alone crying

She knows they all took the test
In hopes leaving was best

They've traveled far but reached nowhere
For there was no brother to care

Not another soul was on that boat
None to steer it but t'was fully afloat

Through tears Ning Lam scans the sea
For what her tomorrow night be

Her name is My-Neng and she's on a boat
With a hundred others it can hardly float –

7
Star Burn

Quezon City/Antipolo, 1976-1977

Every story of fame and fortune has to start somewhere, and I would blame this one on my woodgrain portable Zenith with the halo antenna and bad reception. It was a hand-me-down when my parents traded up. To stop the staticky reception, I repeatedly repositioned it in my bedroom. After all, I had an addiction to feed.

I was nothing short of euphoric flipping through my copy of *TV Times* on which I splurged my weekly allowance. Every night, even if I had not finished my homework, I sat in front of the small screen, close enough for Mommy to warn I would go cross-eyed, as if I was not already with my wandering left eye.

Most of my diet consisted of American shows popular in a country my parents said that after three hundred years in a Catholic convent thanks to the Spaniard colonizers, was followed by fifty years in Hollywood. Won along with Cuba, Puerto Rico, and Guam in the Spanish American War, the Philippines, after decades of a love and hate affair with the United States, was granted independence in 1946. Yet U.S. culture remained pervasive long after, including its main medium, television.

While I enjoyed *Little House on the Prairie*, *The Waltons*, and *All in the Family*, I was partial to *The Six Million Dollar Man* and *The Bionic Woman*. I wanted to be a star like Lee Majors and Lindsay Wagner. I fantasized about adoring fans who were like paper clips drawn to a magnet. I'd see myself bestowed accolades at glitzy award shows. I would stride up to the podium to give my acceptance speech and thank my parents, family, and friends. Anyone who believed in me. Even those who doubted me.

It was a Saturday in late June, just before the Giaos left for America, when I stumbled upon the premiere telecast of *NewsWatch: Junior Edition*, a thirty minute spin-off from the nightly grownup edition. It was interspersed with interview segments and was co-anchored by two boys and two girls. It ran weekends on RPN-9, the top-rated network and a political vox to the Marcos regime.

"Tatay, can you drive me to the TV station?" He looked up from his desk in his home office and gave me a bewildered look before I could finish my thought. "I want to be on TV!"

He sat back, took a sip of his instant Nescafé, then tapped his ballpoint pen over a folder of newspaper clippings he had been collecting for his next book in his field of Public Administration, before cracking a smile.

"Okay, how about tomorrow afternoon?"

How about tomorrow?!

We drove to the station without an appointment. Tatay dropped me off at the front gate surrounded by barbed wire fencing.

"I'll be here waiting," he said.

I told the military guards with rifles strapped across their chests that I wanted to see the producer of *NewsWatch: Junior Edition*. After they called into the building, stating my name, my age—twelve—and who I wanted to see, I signed into a logbook and was escorted into the lobby. Fifteen or twenty minutes later, a woman with wavy nutmeg hair, Formica teeth, and a laughing smile walked up to me.

"Hi, I'm Fe. Nice to meet you. What is your name again?"

"Jobert, Miss Fe. Jobert Abueva, *po*." I ended with a Filipino honorific.

"Abueva? Abueva, Abueva...oh, just call me Fe."

I followed her up a floating Z staircase to the second floor into a conference room where a man and woman were conferring in a corner.

"Mr. Medina, Mrs. Reyes, this is Jobert Abueva."

Mr. Medina had a silver mane, yellow teeth, a bulky gold wristwatch, and a cross between a limp and a swagger. He extended a hand.

"Nice to meet you, Jobert."

"You too, Mr. Medina."

"This is Mrs. Reyes, head writer of the show," he said. "I'm the director and executive producer, and you've already met Ms. Felisimo, producer." Mrs. Reyes looked like a librarian at my school, with silver-rimmed glasses and a curtain of bangs and short jet-black hair. She was showing maybe halfway through her pregnancy.

"Hi, Jobert," she said. "Is your father National Artist Napoleon or Jose?"

Even at this age, I was keenly aware of my surname's nobility and notoriety and perhaps unconsciously pressured myself to live up to them.

"Dr. Jose, *po.*"

Their eyes widened, and their heads moved in unison toward each other, communicating without words. Mr. Medina asked me to sit down as all three of them sat across the long acacia table, judging committee style.

"So, what brings you in today, Jobert?" asked Mrs. Reyes, her voice sounding less scary.

"I would like to audition for *Junior Edition*. I think I can do well."

"So, your father is Jose, former Secretary of Con-con, yes?"

They were talking about the 1971 Constitutional Convention when a new constitution was in the works before Ferdinand Marcos upended it with martial law. Many delegates who were viewed as dissenters were indeed rounded up and imprisoned, and some even murdered.

"Yes. Mrs. Reyes. That is correct"

"And where is Dr. Abueva these days?"

Why they were so curious about Tatay's whereabouts, I had no idea. I wanted this gig more than anything else. And as Tatay always liked to say, the truth shall prevail.

"Oh, he's waiting in the car outside."

Two days later, I found myself in a dark corner of a broadcast studio, an ice box, as Harry Gasser, a Filipino Dan Rather with a bad complexion, signed off with his staccato English delivery of the evening news. Even as he yanked off his headset and stepped away from his desk, his face remained tight with a pout and a frown. He was so much shorter in real life. He walked right past me without acknowledging my presence. I wanted to say something, but the moment had passed. He had already pushed through the flap doors under the red EXIT sign as he took off his suit jacket.

Fe, who was also present, asked me to step on the platform and take a seat where Harry Gazzer was a mere minute ago. The chair was still warm with his body heat. The spotlights made me squint. I could not see Mr. Medina, Mrs. Reyes, or Fe. I could not even make out the cameramen who were still present. Lanelle, who drove me to the TV station, was waiting right outside. I looked into a teleprompter, but the words were scrolling by too fast to read. As they adjusted the speed setting, I used my mouth to fog breathe onto my eyeglasses, then wiped them with my shirttail.

I twitched as the microphone amplified my testing count from one to ten as well as backward ten to one. I had never heard myself sound like this before. An echo, two of me speaking simultaneously. I cleared my throat, adjusted my posture, and smiled into the camera as Mommy had coached me to do so the night before.

They had me read a report on stamp collecting, which I had recalled from the show I saw. Mr. Medina asked me to look to my left, then to my right, then he came up to me and said I should come back in a couple of weeks, on Saturday morning at eight a.m. for makeup, followed by taping.

"Have someone pick up the script on Friday afternoon after four."

I barely got out the words, "Thank you." But I was flushed, wanting to shake everyone's hand. Fe handed me a large, brown envelope which was my contract to be reviewed and signed by Tatay or Mommy. Mommy was the one to do so.

A routine soon took hold of my weekends. Lanelle picked up my script after her last Friday class at the U.P. I practiced my two assigned news stories in front of Mommy. I was bleary-eyed as Lanelle and I left home for the TV station no later than six thirty in the morning. Makeup seemed to last a very long time. The artist did not speak a word as she pancaked my entire face with foundation before applying pink lipstick and eyeliner.

"Don't wear blue next week," Miss Fe said. They used blue to project other images as backdrops on screen. An interview guest once wore the forbidden color, and all we could see was a floating head on the monitor. They had to bring him out an extra shirt.

After a breakfast of hot chocolate and cheese and sugar coated bun ensaymada they made available on set, taping started around nine thirty, sometimes ten, and would run until two or three in the afternoon. There was a lot of waiting time between segments. The show ran at five thirty on Saturday evening, with a repeat at two on Sunday afternoon. My family watched the Saturday show. I watched both.

My co-anchors were Rina Reyes, Dolly Carvajal, and Andre Castillo. We were all around the same age. They looked at me like I came from another planet when I first joined.

"What happened to the other boy who was here last week?" one of them asked.

Rina was the daughter of the actress Baby O'Brien and granddaughter of the legendary post World War II actress Paraluman, who along with a doting yaya, accompanied Rina to every show taping, as if they were on a picnic. They had folding chairs, an ice chest full of soft drinks, a first aid kit, and a change of clothes.

Once I got into trouble with Rina's lola when I wanted to use a new word I had just learned in class. Our English teacher advised us to use new words as often as possible in conversation. As soon as I off-handedly observed that Rina looked "sensual" in her red dress, her grandmother raised her voice at me.

"Don't use that word ever again."

The glower from beneath her tight bun left my forehead singed.

Rina would eventually be known as a sexy actress in B movies.

Dolly was the daughter of Inday Badiday, whose stage name seemed to encapsulate her essence. She was the top-rated talk show host of *Truth or Dare*, which always had the juiciest celebrity gossip. After our own tapings, I sometimes joined Dolly to visit her mom on the set of her program, which went live on Saturday afternoons.

Years later, Dolly would eventually follow in her mother's footsteps with her "Hello Dolly" column, a sort of celebrity and showbiz "Page Six" in *The Philippine Inquirer*.

The third host, Andre, did not seem to have a direct tie into show business. At least that's what I thought. He may have been related to someone associated with the network. He always left soon after we finished taping, to attend singing and tap dancing classes. He later on would be part of a popular singing group, The Company.

I was the politico's son. Past Secretary to the Constitution Convention. Perceived opposition to the regime. My family would discuss the stories assigned to me at dinner.

"They give him all of the pro-Marcos bullshit," Lanelle blurted out one Friday night.

"What can you do?" Tatay replied.

"All your friends are laughing," she said. "It's so obvious they're using the Abueva name."

"I really like the show, and they're good to me," I countered.

"That's all that matters," he said.

What a thrill it was when I was asked to sign my first autograph while shopping for school supplies at National Bookstore two weeks into my job. Tatay would browse textbooks and the Filipiniana section, pretending not to notice what was going on.

Soon I was signing autographs and posing for pictures at grocery stores, after Mass, at the parking lot in school, and at friends' birthday parties. Not long after, Tatay, Mommy, and I drove by a newly opened Jobert's Custom Tailoring. We even saw a Jobert's Taxi. There would soon be a crop of Joberts born around the same time period when I was on air.

Sometimes Lanelle and I had pizza at *Italian Village* near the TV station after a show taping before we headed home. I signed a menu that they hung along a wall of fame photo and autograph gallery. Once when I washed my hands in the restroom, our waiter followed me. I did not think much of his friendly banter while standing by the urinal until he started stroking his penis.

"Come here. Want to play with it?"

I slicked my hair with my palms and briskly walked back to our booth. I did not look his way when he brought out the pizza and later the bill. I did not want anyone to know this side of me existed. But did the waiter see through me? Or was it the makeup I had yet to wipe off my face that made me a welcome mat for his advances? The last thing I needed was a scandal, and to be a headline on Inday Badiday's show.

My appearances led to voiceover work for radio commercials. I met celebrities, while roaming the studios and hanging out in the green room at Dolly's mom's show. We were nominated for a PATAS, the Filipino equivalent of an Emmy. Of all the co-anchors, I was the only one who attended the awards dinner, unchaperoned. Tatay had dropped me off at the Meralco Theater where it was broadcast live. We won Best Children's program, but only Mr. Medina and Mrs. Reyes went up to accept the award. Neither one thanked any of us co-anchors. I felt robbed for not being acknowledged and wondered if the others felt the same way as they watched from home. I never bothered to ask any of them.

The life I had fantasized about had become reality. I was a bona fide celebrity in my mind. And having my own cloud to sit on and see the world from, I found it easier to be nice to others. I anticipated someone somewhere would recognize me where ever I went. At the time I was too immature to understand that my hungry ego was on a constant hunt for attention calories.

Then the monsoon season arrived. It was late June of 1977, and I had been on the show for over a year.

After dinner one evening Tatay announced he had taken a position with the United Nations University. We were moving to Tokyo.

He looked my way, expecting a reaction. He must have rehearsed this.

"I don't want to go," I said. "I want to stay here. I can study here."

"Jobert, that's not how it works. The whole family is going."

"I don't want to." I folded my arms into a knot. I did not know where to run to, but I had to escape somewhere. My chair scraped away from the table as I headed for the stairs and turned to my family yelling, "you can't make me do this."

"Come back here," Tatay said.

I remained atop the staircase. "Why are you taking this away from me?" Tears streamed down my face and onto my hands and shirt. "I worked hard for this. You let me do it. I hate you!" I then ran up to my room and slammed the door.

No one came after me as I sobbed in bed. I contemplated running away from home. I could wait until everyone was asleep. I would pack light: my school knapsack with a pair of jeans, two shirts, underwear, toothbrush, a tube of Close-Up toothpaste, and the *TV Guide* spread of *Starsky & Hutch*. They were all that I needed to see me through. I would continue to be on TV, yet my family would be unable to locate me. Bodyguards in sunglasses would communicate via walkie-talkies escorting me everywhere I went. Never mind that I was being used to spew propaganda on behalf of a dictatorship.

In August of 1977, I completed my sixtieth taping of *News Watch: Junior Edition*. The cast and crew seemed sorry to see me go. Staring into David Soul's eyes could not soothe my heart of pins. A blue and white "Good Luck Jobert" cake from Goldilocks Bakery was cut. Coke and Royal Tru-Orange soft drinks overflowed. Photos were snapped. And just like that, I departed for Tokyo the following week.

8

Supply and Demand

Kyoto, 1977

I was the first son. Dubbed the Great Expectation after eight years of my parents trying to have a second child. Top of the heap within sibling rivalry. The special one. Whatever I put my mind to, I came out a winner. I was boy wonder. But...

Aray! (Filipino) Itai! (Japanese) Ouch! (English).

For the tenth time in three minutes, I pushed my throbbing lobster red palms off the ice to stand up again. Still wobbly, I raised my arms as if I was about to step onto a high wire, only to panic, making wild windmills and landing back on my butt. Fall number eleven.

"Make it like you're walking!" Tatay shouted from behind the barrier. His inky eyes were shielded by aviator bifocals that stretched from ear to ear beneath his wide forehead and receding hairline. He was coach, judge, and peanut gallery.

"Don't tell me what to do," I muttered.

I was too unnerved to get one skate in front of the other and required another four-hand push by Rossana and Jonas. *Showoffs.* My now eleven-year-old sister and ten-year-old brother were completing circles around me. Coordination and daredevil gusto, both with Scorpio traits this jealous Pisces despised. They had curly hair and sibling simpatico. I, on the other hand, at thirteen, had wavy hair, still with my lazy left eye and black nerd glasses which left indent marks on my skull. Their eyes seared me with ridicule as I fell yet again. Fall number twelve. I was determined to find my footing. Never mind that the skates choked my ankles, cutting off circulation, my toes prickling in pain.

Shit. Fall number thirteen. Tatay shook his head as he looked down. So did Mommy seated in the bleachers with Lanelle, now twenty-one years old, who snapped away on her Polaroid. I darted feigned laughter their way then brushed ice shavings off my soaking jeans.

"Jobert, you can do this," yelled Tatay through his cupped-hands megaphone. "Don't worry about the others. Just stay focused."

"Easy for you to say," I shouted.

"Don't give up."

"Go away."

"Stay focused."

Shut up.

The days that led up to our first New Year's in Japan were coated with brushstrokes of grey, a stubborn overcast in the land of the rising sun. Tatay had gone ahead of us to Japan for his administrative position at the United Nations University headquartered here. We followed at summer's end: Rossana and Jonas weeks ahead of me, Lanelle and Mommy weeks after me.

By then, my siblings and I had grown accustomed to being uprooted from school and away from newfound friends for the sake of being together as a family. In four years, we had relocated from Manila to Kathmandu to Bangkok then back to Manila. And now Tokyo. Still, every move was a disruption, a tremor building up to some significant shift. Moreover, my Filipino celebrity currency devalued to centavos on the peso the moment I exchanged it for Japanese yen. I had to establish myself all over again.

I was surprised if not perplexed to find us here. At family reunions, Tatay, along with his siblings, reminisced as children of World War II when Japan occupied the Philippines. They told tales of trauma through humor. My favorite was of their grandparents who had their custom-made coffins carried by household help "just in case" as they fled to the hills.

His family had lived on the Visayan island province of Bohol where my grandfather was a governor, and both he and my grandmother were leaders of the guerrilla movement. They were executed by Japanese soldiers after Douglas MacArthur had returned and just days after the war was declared over. Sixteen-year-old Tatay, nicknamed Pepe, and a cousin—had found their bullet-riddled bodies and were left to break the news to their four siblings. Tatay's brother, Napoleon, known to us as Tito Billy, the National Artist sculptor, had been tortured previously. Emotional scars ran deep. So much so my titos and titas were taken aback by Tatay's decision to take us here. He claimed it was a once-in-a-lifetime opportunity. Yet here we resided, in the heart of still enemy territory, and every man I passed who may have been old enough to have shot my grandparents was suspect.

Mommy grew up an orphan. She was only two when both her parents died of heart attacks, leaving her and four siblings to be passed around like a ticking time bomb game among the relatives. Knowing this has helped me roll her insecurities and idiosyncrasies off my shoulders. She showed her love through good if not obsessive compulsive housekeeping. Dust bunnies never outran her. And every school morning, my blazer, blue knit tie, white shirt, and grey trousers hung pressed in the bathroom. As for sifting through my belongings, even my diary, I had to stay steps ahead of her to keep her out of my business.

All her provocative bikini poses in the stacks of washed out colored photos I once uncovered in Tatay's home office signaled a siren. Her long, jet black hair and high cheekbones had mesmerized him when he had first laid eyes during course registration at the University of the Philippines. She had been a student and he, an assistant professor.

So, I never knew my grandparents and could not relate when others spoke of theirs. All I had to imagine what my lolo and lola were like was their black and white wedding portraits, in which they wore expressionless stares which left little to decipher. As for my parents, I could not imagine life without them. In contrast, they played to the camera in sepia tones, movie stars about to live happily ever after.

They were my idols. I wanted them to love me. I wanted them to be proud. Their approval was my life's mission. Every 'Most Responsible' or 'Most Courteous' ribbon or Top Ten class rank certificate as far back as Grade One was mounted in Mommy's scrapbook. These, along with her tendency to overshare my achievements with others, were the metrics by which I knew I was on track. And unlike the others, I had never been spanked.

I was the goody two-shoes of the bunch. And was damn proud of it.

However new things were going on with me I dared not reveal. Hair grew like grass at the base of my penis, wiry and creepy. I slept with Kleenex tissues between my thighs so I would not wake up with that stickiness, that smell of Clorox on my pajamas which Mommy would have sniffed out as she scrutinized the laundry. In eighth grade, I had been removed from the soprano section and relegated to the croaking altos.

Christmas, while a holiday elsewhere, was a regular work day. The popular custom was to dine on a barrel of Kentucky Fried Chicken as well as strawberry shortcake. So, we did. The day after, we boarded *Shinkansen*, the bullet train, at Tokyo Station and two hours later arrived in Kyoto, the ancient capital. It was off-season, and only a handful of sightseers ascended the damp stone stairway to Kinkakuji, the sixteenth century Golden Pavilion at the foot of the mist-masked hills. Its façade was placid except for a lone crane, whose wings flapped like ribbons, momentarily soaring before crashing into the water of a nearby lake, causing sloppy ripples. It called out its grating cry perhaps to others nowhere to be found.

We sipped green tea from clay cups, bits of leaves clinging to our tongues. We ate broiled eel in sweet sauce to keep our blood warm. But the highlight was ice skating, which we discovered at our Holiday Inn. It was Rossana's, Jonas's, and my first time in a rink, and we had it all to ourselves.

My body crumpled. Fall number fourteen.

"Time out," I said, panting. "I need bigger skates."

My ego bruised, I wanted to regroup. I needed to pee. As I struggled to yank off my left skate in the men's locker room, I noticed a man standing over a sink washing his hands. We locked eyes through our reflections in the mirror. I had no clue of his age, though he looked older than Tatay. His hair was white, and his upside down triangle face was pink and blotchy. He wore a black, long-sleeved shirt buttoned up to his chicken neck and tucked into belted black pants.

Like me, he was what the Japanese called gaijin, a foreigner, but he was the more recognizable kind—Caucasian.

I turned to massage my arch before sneaking a glance back his way. *Oh my god, he's still staring at me.* He jerked a nod as if to say, "come over here, I won't bite." He then backed away from the sink and pulled out a thousand yen bill from his shirt pocket. I searched his cloudy eyes, glazing over the crisp bill. He snapped it before putting it away, this time in his pants pocket.

"Come to my room," he said. He dangled a room key with the numbers 8-1-1. "Got it? Room 8-1-1."

I turned silent, stiff like the rocks of a Zen garden. He walked away without taking his eyes off me, nodding vigorously before disappearing.

I looked at myself in the mirror and felt a rush of warmth overcome my face. The throbbing in my palms had jumped to my temples. I wiped my hands over my forehead, down to underneath my glasses to rub my eyes, then back up to my scalp. *What to do?*

In minutes, I walked down the frayed moss carpeting past flesh-hued doors. *802. 803. 804.* A lemony stench made me wince. It was extra sharp and sweet, as if to neutralize something putrid. *806. 807.* I pondered the many doors and what unfolded behind those "Do Not Disturb" signs. Even empty rooms must have had stories to tell. *808. 809. 810.* All the doors we pass in life, never knowing what awaits us, never fully understanding what leads us to one and not the others.

811. The door was ajar. I took a deep breath.

"You made it," the man said, cracking a sort-of-smile as he double locked the door behind me.

The heater was whizzing, blasting on high. He unbuttoned his shirt and laid it on a chair by the drawn curtains. Salt and pepper chest hairs burst out of his V-neck undershirt, his arms bony and skin flaking.

He walked up to me, took my clammy palms and guided me as if we were about to waltz. I was so hot. Boiling from within. I started to itch. *Why don't I resist him?* We moved between the two single beds, one of them turned down with a green foil-wrapped mint atop a doorknob breakfast menu.

"Come closer," he said.

I stepped forward, stopping short of pressing against his belt buckle. He grabbed me around my butt. His tongue, like a lizard's, darted for mine. His breath was sour, so I turned away with a grimace.

"Take your pants off."

"I don't think I can."

"I said take them off."

He pushed me aside and returned to the chair where his shirt was hanging. He unbuckled his belt, stepped out of his trousers, and folded them over the chair as meticulously as he had his shirt. He returned with his penis hanging out the fly of his cornflower blue boxer shorts.

He began to stroke it. It was wrinkled and loose and etched with violet veins.

"At least make me come," he said.

I wanted to escape, but something compelled me to see this through. *Yes, I walked through the door.*

He rested his left arm over my shoulder, and pulled me in, sinking his face into my scalp, pushing and pulling with force. I looked up at his shut eyes. He tightened his grip on me.

"Oh, god," he grunted as he pulled away and spurted semen on the starched bedsheet. Once, twice, followed by droplets onto the carpet. He released my shoulder and gasped for air. I stepped aside, nearly tripping over a bed corner.

"So, do I get the money?" I was surprised to hear myself ask.

"No," he said gruffly as he wiped himself off with a towel. "You didn't do what you were supposed to."

I sighed, somewhat confused. Part of me was horrified for having asked about the money. Part of me was downright angry, thinking I'd earned the cash for following him to his room. I walked toward the door and turned around to see him button back his shirtsleeves. He knew I was watching him, but he ignored me anyhow.

I slammed the door and walked twice as fast back to the elevator as I had coming in. *Shit. Why did I not get the money?*

"Where were you?" Tatay asked as I stepped back on the ice with the same pair of skates. Rossana and Jonas were now racing around the entire length like speedskaters.

"I got lost." It may have sounded unconvincing, but how far from the truth had I really strayed?

"Are you all right?"

"I'm fine. I want to try again."

He smiled. Only this time it was a 'that's my boy' sort of smile.

I glided past my brother and sister without losing my balance, without falling on my butt. I picked up speed, in full control, and arrived at the other end before grabbing on to the barrier. Something profound had woken up inside of me. There was nothing I could not conquer.

"You did it," Tatay cheered, his arms straight up as if I had scored a touchdown. Rossana and Jonas gawked in disbelief while Mommy and Lanelle gave me a standing ovation.

Oo! Yatta! Hooray!

But what the fuck was going on?

9

Akemashite Omedetou:
Happy New Year

Tokyo, 1978

Tatay shook us out of slumber like packs of sugar before they were torn open and poured into hot steaming coffee. We were back in Tokyo from Kyoto, but it was too early in the morning on New Year's Day. Even the sun was not up yet. The glow of the kerosene heater in the matchbox room Jonas and I shared had waned into a cold, bluish halo.

We had gone to sleep soon after midnight, disappointed the Japanese did not welcome New Year's with the cacophony and revelry we were accustomed to back in the Philippines. I loved to shop with my family for fireworks named after the explosions they emanated: Spinning Wheel, Bazooka, and the Belt of Judas with its successive staccato of one hundred pops before a big bang at the end. My siblings and I always looked forward to the lost finger count on the next day's news report.

Instead, we huddled in front of the TV to watch Shinto priests bong the grand bell with mindful intent 108 times to wash away humankind's 108 sins at Meiji Shrine in Central Tokyo, while people clapped their hands twice before folding them together and bowing in prayer for good fortune. I, too, observed my own moment of silence, resolving to get good grades, to make more friends at St. Mary's International, my new school, and to avoid doors like Room 811 at the Holiday Inn in Kyoto.

"Boys...snow," Tatay said with excitement, his remaining strands of hair pillow-styled into attention.

Jonas and I jerked up out of our futons. We scurried into the living room where Mommy, Lanelle, and Rossana were already up, kneeling on the couch in various states of wonderment, as if an apparition of the Blessed Virgin Mary had appeared before them. We joined them to look out the glass mural onto what was usually a stone path, as well as our neighbor's roof. On clear days, we could see many more roofs below that, leading to the verdant baseball diamond and training ground of the perennial penchant-clinching Tokyo Yomiuri Giants. I would soon become a huge fan, collecting the autographs of greats like homerun king Sadaharu Oh, team manager Shigeo Nagashima, and many others, as I awaited them to exit the clubhouse after practice.

But on this magical morning, as the clock on Tatay's desk read 4:55, flakes fell like flour through a giant sieve in the sky, frosting the naked cherry tree in our yard and blanketing all of the darkness around it four, maybe five inches deep.

Rossana and Jonas were spellbound. It was their first snow. I felt like it was mine as well, but our Super 8mm home movies proved otherwise. However, I had no recollection of walking shoulder deep in the Connecticut snow that Christmas of 1966, when we had visited Tatay's brother, Tito Teddy, who lived in Manhattan but happened to have a cottage for the winter in New Milford. Santa had left me a DC6 model airplane that year. Most of the reels from then showed newly-born Rossana crying and everyone else making funny faces at her while pointing to the camera. There was a brief scene of me holding her milk bottle vertically, thinking no one was watching, and it caused her to gag and spew milk from all sides of her mouth. Every time I watched these home movies, I was acutely aware that by being born in Brooklyn, Rossana was an American, and I, a Filipino.

But I was fairer-skinned than any of my siblings. Mommy said there was French and Portuguese in her blood. Tatay said Spanish in his. To others, I looked Chinese, Japanese, Thai, Malaysian, Eurasian, anything but a typical Filipino. I was a chameleon. I fantasized I was adopted but saw too much of myself in Tatay: his wide forehead, bookish demeanor, and giddy curiosity about the world, evident in his need to wake up us all the minute he saw snow as he got up to go to the bathroom.

"Can we go out and play?" asked Jonas.

"Can we, can we?" echoed Rossana.

"It's too early," said Mommy.

"Maybe later when there's daylight," added Tatay. "Let's go back to sleep."

They eagerly headed back to bed on his promise. I reluctantly shuffled behind. Under the covers, I was unable to close my eyes. I wanted to walk outside while the world was still asleep and the snow pure. At least before Rossana and Jonas did so.

I waited until my brother exhaled whistle-like breaths before I fumbled in the dark for a pair of jeans, which I put on over my long johns. I layered three T-shirts under a Michigan hooded sweatshirt Tatay brought back when he last visited his alma mater. I pressed the light button on my silver Seiko chronograph wristwatch I had received for Christmas. It read 5:40. I slipped into a grey parka, slid on black mittens, and tiptoed to tie my sneakers in double knots in the vestibule, as Mommy would expect me to, thus maintaining the sanctity of a shoe-free Japanese home.

I plodded up the one-lane street we lived on. My steps crushed the snow, squeaking like the wooden floors meant to mimic the cooing of nightingales in the palace in Nara we had visited, not far from Kyoto. The donut holes stamped into the concrete for traction were buried beneath. A signpost at the bottom of the hill noted a thirty degree incline. Above it was a concave mirror to help drivers overcome the blind spots of narrow streets. In Tokyo, caution was a full-time preoccupation.

From the top of the hill, I turned around to marvel at my meandering, snake-like path. I was a Sherpa on the summit of Everest. I had made the first track marks on the first snowfall on the first day of the year. Its significance filled my small chest as I exhaled with force, almost a grunt, and saw my breath billow ever so briefly before it evaporated into the frigid air.

I trudged past gated homes, normally cozy and charming under sunny skies, their snowcapped silhouettes stacked over one another. Whenever someone found out my family lived in the leafy residential community of Den-en-chōfu, they gave a curious look and nod of approval, as it was Japan's answer to Beverly Hills, California, as Tatay put it.

It was an upscale neighborhood located in Ota-ku, one of Tokyo's twenty three wards, not unlike Paris's arrondissements. It had a European feel to it with a Swiss-like structure for a train station that looked out into a small rotunda with a man-made pond and circular concrete benches at its center. The Saint Germain bakery was on one end and Kentucky Fried Chicken, the other.

I would respond as if in apology by shaking my head from side to side and saying we were only renting, and the United Nations was subsidizing our housing. I used the same excuse for our left-hand drive Toyota Crown station wagon, reserved for export markets. We had blue U.N. diplomatic license plates. Everyone here thought diplomats believed they were above the law as stories abounded of double parking and running red lights and getting away with it. Having the license plates was both a badge of honor and horror.

Fifteen minutes later, the first hint of day had touched the sky and the snow had halted with stray confetti flakes blowing in the wind. I entered a sloping park the size of a street block halfway to the train station. I could barely make out the contours of picnic tables, swings, and seesaws which were all shrouded in sheets like summer house furniture in the off-season. My toes were numb. I felt wetness creep up my leg and around my knee. But the mystery of the snow and how it lacquered the landscape, urged me forward.

I felt a pinch in my bladder and down to the tip of my penis. It had been building since I stepped outside. I needed to pee. The public restroom was on the opposite end of the park and was too far to reach in time. I ran behind a gingko tree so no one could see me. I shed my gloves and unzipped my jeans, struggling to pull out my putty penis through the trap of my long johns. It was difficult to maneuver with all the T-shirts and sweatshirt bunching over it. It remained stuck. Urine began to dribble out on the fabric. In a panic, I unbuckled my belt, unbuttoned my jeans, and shucked down them and my long johns far enough to release it. A stream gushed. I was overcome with relief. Steam rose from the streaks I cut deeply into the snow. It was art. I imagined my penis was a paintbrush flicking acrylics on a canvas, and I then twisted my hips wildly from side to side. I was making lawn-sprinkler patterns. I was Jackson Pollock.

I looked around, embarrassed at my silliness. No one was with me. No one could see me.

I was still clutching the loose piece of flesh in my hand, my last strokes to strangle out the remaining drips that soon turned into the first strokes of masturbation. I pushed and pulled. It had been weeks since I'd been able to do so with family around continuously throughout the holidays. And long before the Holiday Inn incident when I did not take off my pants for the man with the thousand yen bill.

A Betamax video began to playback inside my head. I had returned to Room 811. He was planting his lips onto mine, his breath still sour. I pushed and pulled faster and harder. I was growing hard, but it was short-lived.

The image was then replaced with that of another, my imagination on overdrive. I was in some room. He was much younger but still older than me. His eyes were lagoon blue—watery with patches of sky trapped inside. He had short blond hair styled like wheat in an open field over his chiseled cheeks and Nordic nose.

I was erect. It hurt, but I felt good.

He held me in his arms like I was the most important person alive. I swallowed my breath, and we kissed.

And a surge ruptured at the head of my dick. An arc of semen spit forth and splotched the snow, and again, and again. It was a creamy mess. A masterpiece.

My family believed how we behaved on New Year's would set the tone for the rest of the year. I also gave credence to going blind if I played with myself too often. And my Catholic religion was not accepting of the practice. But then Santa Claus was still a plausible proposition long after I had to accept otherwise. The point being that pleasuring myself and thoughts of males being so closely associated with each act, well, there was no feeling quite like it. Yet I knew it was best kept a secret. In my reality and fantasy, it was all so inexplicably delicious and leaving me often times delirious.

I retraced my steps home, chuckling to myself, still nervous, not exactly sure why.

10

A Boy Named Paul

Tokyo, 1978

No curse was greater than taming a gaggle of eighth graders. Or so it seemed for our homeroom teacher, Brother Gervais. He wore old lady glasses and the same Mr. Rogers sweater that smelled more like Roquefort cheese with every passing week. While scrawling the day's Bible passage such as Proverbs 3:5-6 on the left corner of the chalkboard, he finger-combed stray spaghetti strands of hair over his tomato scalp and pasted them down with spit. This was our signal to erupt into a desktop lid slam fest until Brother turned around and raised his hands in surrender pleading, "Boys, boys. Stop, stop." We then halted and returned to whatever we were doing as if nothing had happened. But just as he turned his back to us, we started up again.

This always left him hands on hips, dumbfounded as to why we made his life a living hell when we were the sons of diplomats, expatriate businessmen, and families of mixed Japanese heritage—Italian-Japanese, German-Japanese, Brazilian-Japanese, and so forth. Hafus. All supposedly from good homes, seeking the best English language college preparatory education in Tokyo money could buy. I felt sorry for Brother Gervais but knew better than to buck this or any other eighth grade pubescent ritual that predated me, a new arrival at St. Mary's International School.

"Je besoin de timbres" was the first and only phrase I mastered under Brother Gervais's tutelage in Beginners French, mandatory because the Brothers of Christian Instruction hailed from Quebec. It was torture to parrot phrases I had no foreseeable use for, and I couldn't wait to drop French come ninth grade and study Japanese instead, which many of my classmates subversively spoke among themselves given the otherwise English-only policy on school grounds.

"And it's Joe-bert, not Jou-burr," I corrected Brother Gervais every time he called on me. But he always responded with a shrug of the shoulders and a crease of the chin, as if to say, "Oui, oui, but it is so French, no?" It was now February. For five months I had been asking him to pronounce my name properly. I had pretty much given up, knowing it could be worse.

According to Tatay, the days leading up to my birth in March of 1964, were the last remaining days of a cancer patient in Eugene, Oregon, named Egbert S. Wengert. He had been a visiting professor in the College of Public Administration at the University of the Philippines. Egbert and his wife had become dear friends of my parents. When Tatay received word of his passing away, he called Egbert's son, Bert Wengert, to offer his condolence.

"If we have a boy, we'll name him after your father," said Tatay. Hours later, they did.

My full name was Jose Egbert Encarnacion Abueva. Jose Abueva was Tatay's name. Encarnacion was Mommy's maiden name. Jobert became my nickname.

"Egbert! Egghead!" My classmates in first grade tittered every time the teacher called out my name, the first on roll call. They laughed on the playground, using my name disparagingly, while keeping the ball away from me on the basketball court. I came home in tears and asked Mommy to change my name. Somewhere between Manila and Tokyo, I officially became Jobert on my report cards and passport. But the baptism certificate forever remained, Jose Egbert Encarnacion Abueva...Jr.

"I think Jobert is a cool name," said Paul.

Paul was from British Columbia, Canada and was one of the tallest boys in class. He had outgrown his charcoal flannel slacks and brass-buttoned dark blue blazer with the St. Mary's insignia sewn onto the breast pocket. Both had fit him fine back in September. Even his navy blue knit tie was too small and looked more like a noose.

I watched him on the basketball court before homeroom and in the back of the classroom where he sat one row to my left and four desks back. His chestnut hair was neatly trimmed but longer than most. He was a young Paul McCartney. When he smiled, dimples formed on his freckled cheeks from out of nowhere. Ever since returning from Christmas break, I wanted to lick his dimples.

One late February afternoon, I sat across from Paul at the library table next to the window looking out into the dishwater sky. We both tried to complete our homework while still in school to avoid having to lug a heavy book bag home.

I was stunned as he looked up from his chapter on ions, protons, and neutrons, to smile and acknowledge me, and to tell me my name was cool, no less.

"Thanks," I said. Beads of sweat trickled down my neck and tickled my back. "I have yet to meet another Jobert myself." I did not bore him with the story behind my name.

"Jobert, do you play any sports?"

My tongue was in a knot. *Quick, quick say something.*

"Um...I run."

"Really?"

He was so handsome. And he was talking to me. I looked into his fiery green eyes while partly shielding my wandering eye with my left hand.

"Track and field season starts in March," he said.

"It does?" I knew but pretended otherwise. I was not going to try out for the team but that was about to change. I found out back at International School in Manila that I was able to run faster than most of my classmates. "I can do the 400 in fifty four seconds."

Paul perked up and smiled. "Cool. You should try out."

"I sure will."

"I'll be on the high and long jumps myself. Shot put too."

"Great." I momentarily savored our seeming to have struck common ground and found something to unite us through the change of seasons and solidify our friendship over into the summer months. And we would be best buddies for the rest of our lives. I was always getting ahead of myself on such matters.

From that day forward, I was able to greet Paul without feeling awkward whenever we crossed paths in the hallway. Then something odd started to happen, not unlike what I recalled with other boys before. Paul appeared everywhere: in the library, in the cafeteria, in my notebook doodles, in my diary, and in my dreams. And just as our eyes locked a smidgen too long, I turned away, deflecting the intensity of his gaze and feigning detachment. I was cool. I was to act casual. I was a boy who was not to look at him the way I wanted to.

But Paul dictated my existence from the moment I woke up to the time I fell asleep. Everything I did was through the lens of Paul. Never mind that he seemed clueless to the chaos he caused inside of me.

Paul was the latest in a string of crushes that ran as far back as I could recall. The earliest ones were on cartoon characters: Charlie Brown, Chet from *Wait Until Your Father Gets Home*, Archie from *Riverdale High*. Despite their foibles, they were lovable. I saw some of me in each of them and wanted to be more like them. Then they were replaced by David Cassidy, Donnie Osmond, and Robby Benson, all clean-cut and all-American. But I did not want to share them with mobs of delirious teenybopper girls, so I had added Starsky and Hutch, *The Greatest American Hero*, and most recently, Luke Skywalker, among others, into the mix as well.

My collective boy crushes to date were forming into a puka shell necklace: Julius in Manila, Stephen from Australia at the British Primary School in Katmandu, Robert from Sweden at Ruam Rudee International School in Bangkok, Lars, another Swede, at the International School back in Manila—all good friends of mine. We had spent time together doing boy things, me happy to just be around each of them, knowing there were clear unspoken limits. But they all preceded puberty, Paul, and how his presence pricked pins all over me.

In the mornings before class, as he and others played hoops, I looked past the court at a make-believe grassy hill. I saw Paul and I running from opposite sides, meeting at the top. We jumped up and down, as if on a trampoline, inhaling the pastel sky. We were circus acrobats laughing and shouting, our voices blowing into the valley below. The world was visible to us, but we were hidden. And when the sun yawned its colors over us and it was time to head home, Paul would turn to me and plant a light and feathery kiss on my quivering lips. The sky would be ablaze with stars of fire from Roman candles.

Then the school bell would ring, and it was time for homeroom.

When it came time for Religion class, we were divided into three sections: Catechism for us Catholics, Christianity for the Protestants, and Ethics for everyone else. I couldn't help but feel smug when a handful of us remained in homeroom for Catechism while the rest were banished to other classrooms, though I briefly considered trading in my ties to the church every time Paul left his seat.

Brother André was our Catechism instructor. He was younger than Brother Gervais, maybe in his twenties or thirties and spoke in a French-Canadian accent stirred in molasses. His hair was dark, short, and thinning. He had a nose too big for his sunken cheeks. But I could not look away from the oversized, dark wooden crucifix with Jesus on it which he wore around his neck and over his chest.

Brother André filled our head with Vatican jargon like "canonization" and "transubstantiation." We learned the difference between black and white synod smoke billowing out of a copper chimney through the roof of the Sistine Chapel. I lost a critical point for my team during a Jesus Bowl when I misspelled Eucharist. I forgot the "h."

It was March. I just turned fourteen and we had three weeks to prepare for the sacrament of confirmation. Brother André led us through readings and prayer meditations geared to prepare us spiritually to be sealed with the sign of the cross and the chrism of salvation. This would follow my baptism, first Holy Communion, and first confession, making it four out of seven possible holy sacraments. I was still trying to determine which of the remaining three I would experience in my lifetime: there was anointing of the sick, matrimony, and holy orders, this last one reserved only for ordained priests. Brother André claimed one of us in class would be called to the priesthood, looking my way every time he said it. I played along by smiling and nodding back to ensure my A+ in class.

"And each of you must choose a confirmation name," said Brother. "Choose a saint. Any saint. You have two weeks."

During track practice, the sprinters and middle distance runners completed laps around the street block that circled the baseball field where Paul practiced his shot put throws. I was fast enough to be on the junior varsity line up, vastly increasing my standing among my peers. As I triumphed on the track, so did Paul on the field. We were both rising stars, which the coach kept in mind for when we entered high school and were eligible to compete on varsity.

I synchronized my schedule to Paul's, so we left school about the same time every afternoon after practice. I refrained from stealing a peek at him as he changed in the locker room across from me, fearful he or someone else would catch me gawking at his treasure trail.

None of us eighth graders used the showers. But the high school runners did, and I had seen some of them naked, with various sized dicks, some circumcised, others not, all hairier than mine. I always turned away before someone noticed me.

I typically splashed my face with water, shucked off my running gear, quickly dressed in my uniform, then jumped back to the gym bleachers where I could see everyone walk by toward the exit door.

Paul seemed glad to see me every time and asked if I was heading home, to which I replied, "Sure, why not?" On our way to the train station, we stopped at a Yamazaki bakery for o-ren-ji-jyu-su and a croissant. Then we caught the same train at Kaminoge station that took us four stops to Jiyugaoka station where we switched trains and went in opposite directions. Often, others were with us, an unwelcome safety in numbers. I wanted to have him all to myself.

Brother André said sacraments were outward signs instituted by Christ to give inward grace. I was in search of a sign that would sanctify what Paul and I had. Any sign would do.

"St. Joseph, of course," Mommy insisted.

It was too obvious to be named after the husband of Mary, the father of Jesus, Tatay's and my namesake.

"Our teacher says it should be someone we can look up to."

Mommy stared back at me. Her eyes turned narrow and fierce as if to say, "so what's your point?"

"And besides, Jobert Joseph sounds stupid." *Remember what you did to me the first time around.*

I crawled into my futon, and my mind raced in circles. I could almost trace them in the dark. I thought of confirmation names, track, French, Brother Gervais's hair, the priesthood, Room 811, and snow. Then Paul. My left hand wandered towards my dick, and I began to stroke it, first slow, then faster, as it swelled up satisfyingly in my palm. I was masturbating more vigorously than usual, oblivious to whether Jonas was asleep or not. After having ejaculated into a tissue paper twice, my breathing uneven as I choked a moan, I made a quick sign of the cross before closing my eyes once more and wishing Paul good night.

I was back in the library the next morning looking up saints. I came across an encyclopedia listing hundreds of them. I turned to the index, to "P", to Paul—St. Paul the Apostle.

"And what have you chosen as your confirmation name?" asked Brother André. I looked out the window and saw the trees pregnant with cherry buds that grew riper by the day. It would soon be the Vernal Equinox, the first day of spring, a Japanese national holiday.

"Paul, Brother. St. Paul the Apostle."

"A fine choice. And why Paul, Jou-burr?"

Because he is the sexiest boy in the entire universe.

I cleared my throat and reached deep from within my mind's grab bag. "He sets a good example as one of Jesus's disciples."

Brother André raised his eyebrows. He was waiting for more. "Yes, but how do you see yourself in him?'

"Oh... St. Paul was the greatest missionary of the early church and wrote more books in the New Testament than any other apostle." I took an audible breath. "He went on four missionary journeys that helped spread Christianity." All heads turned to me as if I was speaking in tongues.

"Please continue," urged Brother André, resting his chin on his left palm which rested on his right elbow. He was stifling a smile.

"So, I too have traveled all my life and feel I can spread the word of God, just as Paul did." *Boy, I'm good.*

I was back in the library that same afternoon working on my algebra homework when Paul slapped my back from behind and squeezed my shoulder.

"Cool confirmation name."

"Thanks...how did you know?" I panicked. *What does he know?*

"Saw it on the bulletin board."

"Oh..."

"Now there are two of us."

"Huh?"

"You know, two Pauls."

"Well, it's just a confirmation name." *Yes, we are one.*

Spring was the season of Japan. Overnight, all of Tokyo exploded into a bouquet of cherry blossoms, as if at the abracadabra of some Asian Merlin. Even the heaviest heart could not ignore their allure. For two weeks, heads tilted up at the cheery pink against the clear and consistent blue sky.

There were fewer rush-hour grunts and curses under the breaths of commuters as platform conductors packed us all into train cars as if we were the last scoop to vacuum-pack into a quart of Baskin-Robbins ice cream. The Tokyo Yomiuri Giants training ground had reopened with high hopes for another pennant victory. The Sunday crowds swelled with exuberance out of hibernation and onto the streets and parks. The fashionable set gathered in trendy Harajuku where high school students in their best *Grease* getups, broke away from their college entrance exam-obsessed existence, to let loose in a cacophony of competing boom boxes. All of Tokyo wanted to congratulate itself for having survived another winter.

It was Sunday, April 9th. If St. Mary's was the most modern school I had ever attended, with its primary colored ramps, white box walls, and skylights, St. Mary's Cathedral (no relation) was the most modern house of worship I had ever been inside. It had high, slanting concrete walls and a wood slat ceiling which consisted of humongous hyperbolas and parabolas come to life from the pages of a geometry textbook. Sunlight seeped in, angling from the apex into the shape of a crucifix.

I was with five of my classmates as well as fifty other students, maybe more, from other Catholic schools, Japanese and International, all of us in our respective school uniforms, waiting for Bishop Stephen Fumio Hamao to confirm us. As the line crawled down the aisle towards the altar, I daydreamed of Paul and me walking together as if we were about to be married. The image did not feel right. I was pretty sure men could not get married. But I could see us alone in a church saying something like, "I love you more than anyone else in the world, forever and ever." I could see it. I could feel it. I could taste…

The bishop rested his hand on my forehead like a slab of meat. I did not look up for fear he could read my thoughts. For fear he would ask me to step aside while he conferred with the two priests on either side, and Brother André, looking from the pews, would be called up into a conference. For fear my parents would then be motioned over by Brother André as the priests grabbed me by the arms and dragged me away, kicking and screaming, "Paul, Paul, Paul! I don't care. I love you. I love you," all the way up the aisle and out the doors while everyone looked on, shaking their heads in pity.

"Jobert Paul, I confirm you in the name of the Father, Son and Holy Spirit. Next, please."

"Hey Paul, how's it going?"

I recognized the voice but was slow to figure it was Paul calling me from behind as he followed me toward the library.

"Hi there." I was about to jump out of my skin and just grab him. I did not know how much more of this calm and collected façade I could feign without losing my composure.

"Hear you're running the individual 400," he said.

"Yup. Coach said he had to give my 400 relay and 200 spots to high school students."

"Cool. I had to do the same with shot put. That's how good we are."

"Congratulations on long run and high jump, though."

"Thanks. Gotta run. See you at the meet?"

"See you at the meet." My voice trailed off into a semi-dreamlike state.

This was typical of our exchanges throughout the season, until the championships in late May. The days had grown longer, as had the training sessions, especially for runners, so I did not get to leave school with Paul as often.

Our last track meet was at Zama, an American military base. All twenty or more of us were on a ninety minute school bus ride early on a Saturday morning. There must have been eight or nine international and American base schools represented and close to two hundred people at the meet. Summer sunshine had arrived, and many of the boys were shirtless in the bleachers. So was Paul, sprawled a few feet away from where I sat. He had finished his events early. I didn't know how he performed, but I could tell from his shirtless sun worship pose he was glad the season was behind him. I slow-eye trailed the thin line of hair just below his belly button running down to the ruffled waistband of his electric blue shorts that read *St. Mary's Titans*. His abdomen glistened. I was left staring at his crotch but snapped out of it realizing I was in public. I looked around to make sure no one had seen me. I had my race to prepare for.

As I set my starting block on the dirt track, all I could think of was Paul following my every move from the bleachers. I shook my nerves out of my arms, neck, and legs, but my hands still trembled as I crouched into position, grit digging into my fingertips.

"Runners on your mark." *This is for Paul.*

"Set..." *This is for us.*

The gun went off, and I spurted down the track. All I saw was my lane and its chalked borders, my spiked cleats crunching. I couldn't fully form a thought because I was too pumped to get to the finish line, to look good in Paul's eyes. My breaths were clipped, and my heart tightened into a fist.

I didn't gulp for air until I made the final turn onto the homestretch. My legs started to feel like lead, ready to fall off. But the crowd's roar thrusted me toward the finish line.

My head throbbed. That was all I knew. Once past the finish line, I came to a spastic stop out of my lane, then fell to my back onto the track, panting furiously, the sun in my eyes, a stretch in my smile.

I came in second to a high school student from ASIJ, the American School in Japan. I didn't even know what he looked like. I was still too out of breath to congratulate anyone.

My teammates soon surrounded me, and we slapped palms, long before anyone knew to call it a high-five. Paul was the last to do so.

He winked. "Way to go, little Paul."

Little Paul. He called me Little Paul. I wanted to run a victory lap.

At first, the bus ride back to Tokyo was alive with more self-congratulatory chatter. A boombox was blasting "We Are the Champions." But the sun was also tired, having left most of us sunburned and sleepy. Soon, a lot of boys dozed off before considering Saturday evening, full of possibilities. I could hear the faint lyrics of "Stayin' Alive" emanating from somewhere in the rear.

Paul and I were seated next to each other, relegated with the other eighth graders toward the front of the bus, with the very back reserved for juniors and seniors. He was asleep, but his head tilted toward me. *Please fall on my shoulder.* A cocktail of sweat and suntan lotion intoxicated me. I looked out the window, barely able to make out the rice fields and houses that melded into one another just before twilight.

I allowed my thigh to sway with the bus and bump up against Paul. It was a game of dare, but also a game of chance. It was time to make a move and make Paul mine. We had come so far. I wanted to be his and have him do with me as he pleased.

I leaned my thigh against his. We were as close as we had ever been. I let out a long and deliberate sigh, before turning to study the contours of his face.

Paul opened his eyes up at me, expressionless as a palace guard. *Thousand one. Thousand two. Thousand three.* He squinted at me. His once fiery eyes turned frosty, as if to say he knew what I had been up to all season long. Then he repositioned himself away from me, curled up, his hands trapped in his thighs. He was a fetus. And I wanted to die.

When we pulled into school, Paul stepped off the bus without looking my way. I held back, pretending to fumble through my knapsack, letting everyone off before stepping off myself. Instead of heading into the locker room to change along with everyone else, I ran down the hill, toward the train station, like I was back in my race until I was out of breath. *What the fuck is wrong with me?*

Tears streamed down my face. I could not outrun them.

11
Question of the Week

Tokyo, 1979

No one must know. No one must know.

Paul had distanced himself the remaining few weeks of eighth grade. I pined over him all summer long. He did not show up on the first day of freshman year. Nor on the second or third, then I overheard others in class say he had returned to Canada over the summer. No one really knew why.

I could not help but be devastated, tumbling down our imaginary grassy hill and onto a deserted shore. Seagulls pirouetted in the salty air, mocking me with their cries as I bent down to stare at the sparkling sand and crunch its grit with my hands, the remains of my sand castle washed back to sea. We were now on opposite sides of the Pacific, a vast, vicious ocean, our ships never to cross paths ever again.

My class had moved one floor up as well as to the very bottom of the high school totem pole. I tried to act mature in unfamiliar surroundings. I walked through the cacophonous hallways, face to floor. Everyone became a safe blur. I clenched the narrow end of my new three-ring binder in the cup of my palm, careful not to cradle it in my arm the way girls did. It was filled with lined paper divided by block-lettered tabs, one for every subject: English, Geometry, World History, Intro. To Phys. Sci., and Catechism. Japanese being the exception. I painstakingly duplicated the intricate kanji characters for Nihongo—日本語. I also had a new blue Everlast knapsack, a brand many on the track and field team owned.

I concentrated on new subjects, new teachers, new textbooks, and even new friends. I was the only freshman on the school's Brain Bowl team. My strengths were geography, current events, and general knowledge. I joined *The Diplomat*, our school newspaper, as well as the yearbook staff. I ran cross country. I landed an ensemble part in the spring school musical, Showtime '79. By packing my schedule with extracurricular activities, I hoped to forget Paul and not have time to think of boys anymore.

It was the middle of January. So far, so good.

Mr. Hauet was the guidance counselor. He was flagpole tall, with a wide, pink forehead and wavy auburn hair. His black rimmed glasses were always smudgy. His wife taught in elementary school and they had a house on the school grounds. One day he called me out of World History class and into his office overlooking the basketball court and school courtyard.

"Jobert, I'd like you to sit in on a group interview for *The Japan Times*."

I liked what I heard. "Sure...happy to." Anything to get my name in print. To be quoted for saying something profound.

He did not offer any more details, though I did not bother to ask him, either. The fact that he had chosen me to participate was more than enough reward, perhaps an acknowledgment of all the extracurricular activities I was packing into my day.

"Thank you, Mr. Hauet."

"No, thank you. Oh, by the way, are your parents in town?" I did not think much of this.

"Yes," I replied before I returned to class, my head floating somewhere above Tokyo.

I showed up after lunch the following day at the room next to Mr. Hauet's office. It was always locked otherwise. Filing cabinets as tall as me lined an entire wall. I thought it might be where he kept our student records. Six orange plastic chairs, the kind that curved to the body's contours were stacked up, forming a circle in the center. Another wall was decorated with Argus inspirational posters. Rock climbers "Dare to Dream," while a lone runner on a long and winding road pondered, "The race is not always to the swift, but to those who keep on running." That quote would propel me to soldier on whenever I faced adversity or disappointment.

A woman in black boots and white slacks sat cross-legged toward the door. Her head was bowed down and tilted to the left. The bangles on her right hand rattled as she scribbled on her notepad. She perked up.

"Jobert, right? Hi, I'm Maureen D'Honau." She broke into a smile, flashing picket fence teeth, then withdrew all of them just as quickly. "Take a seat. I'm sure the others will be here shortly."

I sat two chairs from her with a clear view of the entranceway. I stared at her unruly black-blue hair, which scraped her shoulders and surrounded her face like a bush in need of trimming. She looked familiar, but I could not quite pinpoint from where I knew her. She resumed jotting down notes on pad paper.

A minute later, four other boys entered the room. I recognized them all: a senior, a junior, and two sophomores. One of the sophomores, an American, was on the track team. The other, an Australian, was in the drama club. I saw him at tryouts for Showtime '79 the week before. The senior, also an American, was on the Brain Bowl team. He recognized me and nodded. The junior was another American. He ignored me and shook hands with Ms. D'Honau. I was trying to figure out why we had been asked to participate and what we all had in common. *One of these things is not like the others* popped into my head. I was the only Asian. Everyone else was white. Ms. D'Honau had everyone take a seat.

"Well, thanks for coming," she said. "I write the Question of the Week column."

Of course. I had been reading her column every Sunday since arriving in Tokyo. She answered queries gaijins had about practical matters such as where to find amenities they miss from back home, like where they can buy A1 sauce or how to find an English-speaking dentist. She also asked peoples' opinions on current events. *How do you feel about moving Tokyo's International Airport from Tokyo to Narita, over two hours away?*

"I enjoy your column," said the thespian sophomore.

I rolled my eyes inside my head. *Kiss ass.*

"Thank you. So, this week's question is who should be educating you about sex?"

Sex. The word rattled in my head (*a-ha, that's why Mr. Hauet didn't offer any details*) before it plopped and settled to one side like a coin that had lost its spin.

The junior chortled. The American sophomore was about to burst into laughter but stifled it and apologized. Ms. D'Honau was already taking copious notes. I waited for others to speak.

The Aussie actor with the tight golden curls and a permanent pout cleared his throat. "Well, all the technical medical stuff should be taught in school while the basic stuff should be done at home."

"What do you consider basic stuff?" she asked.

"My mum just gave me a book 'cause she didn't know what else to do."

You did not answer the question, jerk.

Ms. D'Honau did not say anything as she shifted her crossed legs. She was not looking up from her notes. All I could make out were squiggles.

She startled me with her darting eyes. "Jobert, do you think getting a book is a good idea?"

I scanned the group to see everyone's eyes fixed on me. *Act cool.*

"I'm sure good books are available," I replied. All I could think of was Mommy's copy of *Coffee, Tea, or Me* about the escapades of flight attendants, which I doubt counted. For a week I read it at night and returned it to the bookshelf each morning. "But specific questions can't always be answered by books."

"And what would be an example?"

I took a deep breath. "Let me think." I drew a blank on whether to dodge or dare a response.

"Well, we'll come back to you."

Good. Maybe she'll forget, and I'll be off the hook.

The other sophomore raised his finger. He was in his maize and blue letter jacket, with three golden bars over the entangled S and M of St. Mary's, one for each varsity letter he had earned. His dark brown hair was parted in the middle and covered his ears. "Growing up in Tokyo allows you to grow up faster than back home in the US, because you hang out with guys and girls from different ages."

She uncrossed her legs and sat up straight, nodding every few seconds, like a wooden bird toy that repeatedly wetted its beak into a glass of water.

"Yes, but how do you learn about what's involved in sex?"

I was thinking of the old man at the Holiday Inn. But no way in the world would I have shared that story. It would have been suicide.

The same sophomore continued. "Well, younger boys learn from older boys." *Or older men.* "That makes for a more sophisticated group."

"Perhaps parents need to take courses on how to instruct their own children," interrupted the junior.

Ms. D'Honau seemed less impressed with his comment but jotted it down anyway. She then turned to the senior who had not said a word. He had been soaking in the discussion with his ankle resting over his knee, and his noodle arms folded. "And what are your thoughts?"

His voice was soft and steady. "Although we all feel pretty knowledgeable on the subject, not all of us have experienced it firsthand. I doubt most people in school would admit to having had sex even if they did."

I looked into his cement grey eyes. He was right, and I puffed my chest out in agreement. He was looking straight at Ms. D'Honau, who was still nodding away.

I wanted to blurt out that I'd had sex. At least I thought I had. But she shifted the discussion to what should be included in a sex education class. The others spewed out subjects I always thought to be taboo: circumcision, menstruation, hymens, birth control, condoms, herpes, oral sex, and abortion.

"Don't any of you have questions about homosexuality?"

I held my breath. *Remain calm. Remain cool.*

"A gay just couldn't make it in our school," said the sophomore jock. "He would have a very tough time."

The other sophomore and junior nodded in agreement.

"But couldn't there be gay students at St. Mary's?"

They stole glances at each other as if to say, "is she serious?"

"Well, if there are any, they better keep it to themselves. I don't think they would be too welcome here," said the junior.

His comment angered me. I looked at the senior to say something wise and sensitive. He was staring out the window as if he hadn't heard the question. *Shit, what should I say?*

"Then why do I overhear students call each other gay in school?" Her tone was a bit more emphatic.

"That's just joking around," said the sophomore jock.

She turned to me. "Jobert, anything else you want to add?"

Anything to add? What does she mean? My heart was palpitating, and my throat had gone dry. I wanted this discussion to cease.

"No...they're right."

Her eyebrows bent down in disappointment, and she returned to her notepad. *No one must know. No one must know.* I repeated this over and over like a mantra.

"Do you know any gays?"

We all shook our heads and respond with emphatic "no's."

"Okay, that's all I have. Thank you for your time, gentlemen."

The sophomores and junior jumped out of their seats and shook hands with her.

"When will your column come out?" the junior asked.

"In two weeks. February 4th."

As they headed out I stood up and shook hands with Ms. D'Honau. She did her peek-a-boo smile once more.

"Nice to meet you, Jobert."

"You too."

The senior, still seated, said, "Ms. D'Honau, may I have a word with you?"

We both turned to him. "Certainly," she replied.

It was time for me to leave. But at that moment I sure wanted to stay and find out what he had to say. I begrudgingly left the room.

She called out. "Jobert, please close the door, will you?"

After doing so, I walked into the restroom across the hall before returning to science class. All the tension in my body gushed out as I peed. When the last drip dangled out of my dick, followed by a shiver, I scrunched my shoulders and heard them pop. I then zipped up my pants, washed my hands, and looked at my face in the mirror. I rubbed my eyes under my eyeglass frames. I was still in one piece. I re-looped my belt one hole in, to feel its tightness against my stomach. I creased out my wool pants, straightened my back, and walked out the door.

No one must know. No one must know.

It was early Sunday morning, February 4th when I woke up and ran to retrieve *The Japan Times* from our mailbox. But Tatay and Mommy, he in his bathrobe and pajamas, and she in her night kimono, were already reading it over mugs of coffee.

"Congratulations, Job," said Tatay.

Mommy handed me the *Question of the Week* already clipped and pasted on bond paper with my name and quote about finding information in books underlined. I wanted to surprise them with my name in the papers, but they already knew about it. *Thanks, Mr. Hauet.* I read the entire article. Thrice. There were no surprises. According to Ms. D'Honau, "homosexuality was an area holding little interest for any of them."

My parents and I never discussed sex. Even with the column, we did not broach the subject, just the fact that I had been quoted in *The Japan Times.* Mommy then put the clipping inside a binder with plastic pages, along with my report cards and awards from all my previous schools.

I managed to get out of this episode intact. Nothing was revealed. And it was just as well.

Adventuring

Jobert, high school year book photograph

12
Tea for Three

Tokyo, 1979

I combed the crowd in search of a woman in her fifties, longtime friend of my parents whom I did not know that well but always call her Tita every time I saw her. She was in Tokyo for some academic conference and was coming over to our home for dinner. I saw everyone but Filipinos.

It seemed the whole world had descended upon the Imperial Hotel. I read in the brochure by the housephone that it opened in 1890 at the direction of the Imperial Palace. A Victorian-style structure originally built of wood, it was replaced by a Frank Lloyd Wright design in 1923 to signal the nation's modernity and ties to the West by creating a hybrid of Japanese and Western architecture. But on the day of the hotel's grand re-opening, Tokyo suffered its largest earthquake, killing tens of thousands, but leaving Mr. Wright's structure intact, elevating its stature among structures. It was then replaced in 1970 by the glass and granite grandiosity I found myself in at present.

Still twenty minutes early, I did not call Tita's room to say I was here. Instead, I walked one flight down a staircase into the hotel shopping arcade.

Who saw whom first? I was not quite sure. Yet it happened in a matter of moments: we crossed paths, focused in, and acknowledged our mutual interest with a casual turn over our shoulders.

My head snapped back to face forward. I paused in front of a display—a gold leafed mural screen that folded like an accordion and stood on its own—and gazed at it long enough to imagine the scenery in motion. Women with white Noh complexions and Mona Lisa smiles were laden with flowing kimonos, one serving tea to the other. A ceremony overseen by a burst of blossoms under a springtime sky, not unlike that outside the Tokyo Imperial Hotel on this Saturday afternoon in late March. I had just turned fourteen.

His eyes warmed the nape of my neck. I clasped it, then turned to see that he, too, had stopped three shops down, pretending to window shop Seiko watches and Sony Pressmans, precursors to the following year's Walkmans. His charged stare left no doubts about wanting to make a connection.

He mouthed hello. His teeth were as white and thick as classroom chalk.

I returned a smile before inspecting the arcade's ocha or green tea carpeting. First to the left, then to the right, as if I was about to cross a street. There were few pedestrians around. I looked his way once more. He had closed the gap between us.

"How-are-you?" he asked, like in a beginner's English language tape.

I was mute with nerves. I should have played *me no speak English well,* thus excusing myself from what I was not so sure about, or more importantly, what I had sworn off—following strange men into their rooms. He was in his thirties or forties, with a swath of white thunderbolted through his blown-dry hair. He was Pepe Le Pew. A loose yellow paisley tie dangled over the unbuttoned collar of his button-down oxford. Starch cracks crept up from where his shirt bordered his belt. His sleeves, scrunch-rolled to his elbows, revealed thick, hairy arms.

"Do-you-speak-Eng-lish?"

Here goes. "Yes, I do speak English. And how are you today?"

His mannered smile molded into a devilish grin. "I'm very good," he replied with relief in his voice. "Just doing a bit of shopping." He sounded friendly and smelled of Tatay's Old Spice. By his accent, I was guessing American, but not the twangy kind.

"What'd you buy?" I cocked my head toward two glossy-white bags he carried emblazoned with Mikimoto. *Pearls!* Tongues of white tissue flared from within.

"Oh, just a few gifts for family."

When he lifted the bags, I saw a gold band around his ring finger. An alarm went off in my head.

"How long have you been in Tokyo?" I asked.

"A few days. I come here for work often. Once, twice a month."

"That's a lot of flying. Well, welcome back." *What a lame response.* But what else should I have said? It was not like we knew each other. Yet here we were, standing side-by-side, staring at the mural screen as if waiting for an invitation into the tea ceremony. Our awkward attraction left us dancing around a bonfire of possibilities.

"Listen," he said. "I'm not checking out 'til six. Would you like to come up to my room for a while and relax?"

Relax? I instantly decoded his intentions, although nothing crystallized in my head. I looked at my watch. 4:45. I had fifteen minutes.

"I have to meet a family friend in the lobby upstairs in fif—twenty minutes."

"That's fine. Shouldn't take long. It's room 1212. Twelfth floor.

I was overcome with déjà vu.

"Okay, got it. Go ahead, I'll follow."

He winked and walked toward the elevator banks. I watched him until he turned around and squinted, as if to convince himself I wasn't a mirage. I checked to see if anyone had seen or heard us. Everyone seemed too busy making money, too busy spending it.

I sighed and stepped into the men's room next to the elevator banks to pee and gargle with faucet water. While dabbing my face with a paper towel, I caught sight of my eyes in the mirror. I leaned in and inspected them, my lazy left eye still wandering off. It kept me alert to others' stares, followed by my concluding that they saw something wrong with me, which I viewed as their revulsion and rejection of me as a person.

I pushed my silver-rimmed glasses firmly over the bridge of my nose, tickled the mole over my lip, and stood up the collars of my turquoise Lacoste knit shirt and Levi's denim jacket. All the cool boys in school wore them this way. I was relieved Pepe Le Pew hadn't expressed any reservation over my eye.

It then dawned on me that he had not asked why I speak English well, or where I was from, or what I was doing in Tokyo.

He did not even know my name. Or I his.

I walked one flight up back to the lobby and picked up the faceless hotel phone that connected me to the operator. I wanted to call Tita to say I was running late. There was no answer, and I didn't leave a message. Maybe Tita was already waiting for me somewhere here, maybe in the lobby, but that sort of punctuality would have been atypical for a fellow Filipino.

Guests crisscrossed one another with staccato steps, allegro, as if moving through a morning commute at Shinjuku or Tokyo station. Instead of train cars, they queued up for signs that read Registration, Concierge, Cashier, and even Transportation, ready to make connections whether it was for the taxi line, sunken cocktail lounge, elevator banks, stairwells to the mezzanine, or down to the shopping arcade below.

I sat on a couch where I could spy others entering and exiting the lobby's revolving door and darting in and out of elevator cars. Chain tassels of dark gold dripped from light boxes above, with the same tacky opulence as chandeliers one found at the Hilton, New Otani, Okura, Akasaka Prince, or any of the other top-rated Tokyo hotels. The butterscotch sun beamed through the gossamer of silk curtains that ran to the right of the main entrance. Anyone who sat in the sunken cocktail lounge was smeared with a healthy golden glow.

I was transfixed by a spinning world map, a mural on marble, on the other end of the lobby. Click-click-click-click-click. Continents and islands comprised of tiny metallic cylinders, converted from silver to bronze as the sun supposedly set, and vice versa as it rose, with chronograph. There were also time checks in red LEDs courtesy of Seiko: from Auckland to Bombay to Johannesburg, New York and Honolulu.

A stray thought scratched at me. In this world, someone was always waking up or going to bed, being born or dying, masturbating or fucking.

4:56. *Shit. Room 1212.*

Alone in the elevator, I raced through what could be accomplished in four minutes: a record-breaking mile, the A side of a single, a repeat of the incident at the Kyoto Holiday Inn.

Faced with a time crunch, I asked myself if this was worth pursuing. I felt the erect anticipation against my abdomen and the moist fabric of my Jockey briefs. I examined my denim crotch for any revealing spots.

I can be a little late. No one will know the difference. Trains were running behind schedule, I'll tell my parents.

The doors parted open.

"Going down?" asked a voice. "Jobert!"

I looked up to see Tita entering from the eleventh floor. "Tita, hello! I was just returning from the view upstairs. At the restaurant." I had read of the French restaurant with a majestic view of the Imperial Palace, and I was amazed at how quick I was on my feet.

She oozed of Mommy's Chanel perfume. We kissed in the Filipino tradition, cheek-to-cheek, as the elevator doors shut behind her. We rode to the twelfth floor.

"Hmm...that's strange. I thought this was going down," I said with mild disgust. I pressed the L button repeatedly, as if I was playing Space Invaders—my, and most other boys' after school addiction which was available at any one of Tokyo's hundreds of Ge-mu Sen-tas.

"Were you waiting long for me?" she asked.

"Oh, not at all. Perfect timing." I lit up my Seiko. 5:00. The door pinged open once more, onto the twelfth floor. I took a long deep breath as if to suck the elevator doors back shut.

"I was at the arcade buying pasalubongs to bring home," she said. "You know how it is."

When one travelled abroad, one had to buy presents for friends, coworkers, and just about every member of the family. This was especially the case with the travel ban under Marcos's martial law still in effect. Exceptions to leave the country were rare and sanctioned as was the case with us heading to Japan under the auspices of the U.N.

I was stymied that Tita had foiled my rendezvous with my chance encounter. Then I thought, thank god she had not seen me at the arcade mere minutes ago.

"The subway is downstairs, connected to the arcade. It'll take us thirty minutes to Den-en-chōfu on the Hibiya then Toyoku Line." I had switched to tour guide mode.

"I need to change money at the lobby," she said. "Should only take a minute."

We agreed to meet back by the world map. She lined up for the cashier, at least three or four people were ahead of her. I considered racing back to the twelfth floor to say sorry I can't stay and find out when he might return. But was it enough time? And would I really want to wait for his eventual return when he was ready and willing to do whatever we could do, even in a minute? I took walkathon strides to the house phone and asked the operator to connect me to room 1212. "C'mon, c'mon" I urged the handset as I heard the phone ring. *Shit, no reply.* I hung up just as the operator was about to come back on and tell me the obvious and ask whether I would like to leave a message.

I returned to the world map to see if Tita was still in line. She was counting money at the counter.

Fuck. Game over.

She had spotted me and walked over, with yen bills still in hand.

"I'm ready."

We took the stairs down into the arcade where we headed for the exit that would feed us into the Hibiya subway station and the subterranean network of Japanese punctuality at its finest.

As we were about to turn right at the bottom, I saw him, yes, him, skunk-hair, on the left, making a beeline for the men's room. He did not even see me.

Why is he back down here? What is his hurry?

We continued walking past a Fuji Camera shop and an actual tea store complete with cups, pots, bamboo whiskers, and a tatami straw mat floor. The mind-numbing aroma of green tea escaped into the arcade corridor. I turned to Tita. "I need to stop at the men's room. I'll be right back."

"No problem," she said before entering the tea store where a woman in a kimono had come to life as if from the mural screen. She welcomed her potential customer with a bow and an *Irrashaimase*, the standard welcome at any retail establishment, and seemed ready to drug Tita with some decoction of ocha. Maybe some ginseng, Lapsang, or Souchong.

As I entered the men's room, I saw him washing his hands. Two sinks down, a man with a wide forehead and a bristly mustache did the same. Twenties? Thirties? French? Italian?

Both of them looked up at my reflection in the mirror panel in front of the sinks. I may have ambushed their clandestine deal making. I could hear their nonverbal dialogue loud and clear. I wondered how they were able to make contact so quickly. I walked behind them toward the urinals. I pretended to pee, keeping them within my periphery.

Skunk-hair and I locked eyes, still through our mirror reflections. We seemed to be saying something but were unable to unscramble our signals. *Where were you? Who is he?* Mr. Euro moved one sink next to him and looked up to assess the unwelcome dynamic going on between us.

For Christ's sake, I have a family friend waiting outside.

Just as quickly as we first laid eyes on each other, skunk-hair walked out of the men's room as did the other man I was certain he was picking up. I was left holding my dry dick.

I zipped up in haste and followed them out. They stood side-by-side, though not as if they were together, waiting for the next elevator to arrive. They filed in. First, him, then the other. But the door did not close.

A few seconds later, he stuck his head out to see me looking right back at him. But I didn't know what I was thinking, let alone what I wanted to do. The elevator seemed to remain open for an eternity as if it was an invitation to join them. It didn't close for a good ten seconds, a buzzer exclaiming its loss of patience.

As I was about to head back to the tea store to retrieve Tita, I glanced down the row of shops where he and I had first made contact no more than twenty minutes ago. Many more people were roaming around than before. Somehow, I noticed three, four, maybe more men strolling from store display to store display on either side, window shopping. Their heads bobbed from side to side, checking the others out. Something told me there was more to this arcade than met the eye.

Tita tapped me on the shoulder. "Is everything okay?"

"Of course, Tita. Right this way."

13

Big Apple Bite

Tokyo/USA, 1979

My family and friends were befuddled by my obsession with Japanese pop acts like hitmakers Pink Lady, Machiko Watanabe, Hiromi Iwasaki, and Momoe Yamaguchi. Tatay seemed particularly pleased with my predilection for female artists, a good sign, I surmised, for a son who did not express outward interest in girls. I had classmates convinced that my Japanese proficiency was osmotic proof that marathon listening to silly, saccharine lyrics as well as gluing myself to every music award (Rekoodo Taisho), hits chart (Za Besuto Ten), and variety show (*Koo-haku*) on TV worked wonders.

What I was really doing was wrapping my acne-prone existence in giddy melodies, trying to decipher lyric metaphors of love's ups and downs, pains and pleasures, and how they all applied to me and my secret yearnings.

Japanese pop whetted my appetite for America as well. One of my favorite songs was by a group, Circus (pronounced Sa-kaa-su, and written in katakana, サーカス, as is the case for foreign words), a family act of two men and two women, cousins, whose hit ballad, "American Feeling"—「アメリカン・フィーリング」 (A-me-ri-kan Fi-ring-gu), was the Japan Airlines campaign theme song of the summer. The rousing melody and refrain spoke to cobalt blue skies and the feeling of freedom in America.

The TV ad, accompanied by sweeping aerial images of iconic destinations such as the Golden Gate Bridge, the Grand Canyon, and the Statue of Liberty encapsulated the America I dreamt of escaping to: endless open spaces, center of the universe, prosperity and possibilities. I could be whatever I wanted to be. Land of cowboys and Indians. Marlboro Man.

Ah, I daydreamed of him on his saddled horse, tipping his wide-brimmed hat at the melting sun over the baked canyons. He turned to me, flush right behind him, and asked, "Are you all right?' I dug my fingertips deeper into the denim fabric that shielded his taught tummy, just above the line where his suede chaps and belt buckle met and said, "I'm more than all right." We then galloped off into the fiery sunset, never to turn back. That was enough reason for me to take up smoking along with classmates, but this was short-lived as I couldn't get past the bitter aftertaste of nicotine.

My freshman year was almost over. My sexual urge swelled with every passing day, like a sunburned back in need of simultaneous scratching and soothing. I gave in each night before bed and masturbated to thoughts of Marlboro Man, just another in a still growing list of TV crushes which now included Michael Landon in *Little House on the Prairie*. Never mind he was a father figure who showed his deep affection for Melissa Gilbert and her mom and siblings, dubbed in Japanese. All this in the privacy of my own four and a half tatami mat-sized room, which was supposed to serve as the family tea room although my parents let me annex it for my birthday, providing me with more privacy. No longer having to share a room with Jonas, I was able to sprawl out and make it my own.

On the last night of school in early June, Tatay announced we were off to the United States for summer vacation. He waved a fan of flapping plane tickets. Confetti fell in my head as Rossana and Jonas cheered, jumping up and down as if on pogo sticks. The house shook as it did during the dozen or more earthquakes we had already felt while living in Tokyo. Lanelle had returned to Manila to finish her often travel-interrupted arts degree at the University of the Philippines. Tatay said she would join us on this trip.

"What's the final itinerary?" Mommy asked as if on cue, as if she has known about the trip for quite a while now but wanted to engage in a parental charade.

"Don't worry. We're visiting both your sisters in San Francisco and Chicago," he assured her. "Two weeks starting end of July."

"Are we going to New York?" I asked as Tatay handed me my ticket for inspection.

"Are we going to New York!" he repeated, as if I should have known better.

Like a growing number of Filipinos, our relatives were scattered throughout the United States. The earliest migrants could be traced to before 1776 and continued to arrive in waves with the US winning the Philippines, along with Puerto Rico and Cuba at the end of the Spanish-American War, and as World War II ended. Farmers and sailors and nurses found their way to opportunity as did their immediate families. More recently, relatives looked to follow those who were already settled for what had to be better lives away from the country's rising poverty and now, a stifling Marcos dictatorship.

This trip was an opportunity to see how Filipinos and Filipino-Americans were adapting to their new homeland. In my heart of hearts, I wanted to find a way to live there knowing full well that a permanent line for visa applications snaked outside of the American Embassy every weekday at dawn back in Manila. And that there was a backlog of several years to boot. Tatay and Mommy expressed no interest in living in America, let alone settling there. Tatay said we must all eventually return to the Philippines. For good.

To no one's surprise, Tatay had arranged a jam-packed itinerary which zoomed us through San Francisco, Fort Worth, Chicago, Washington, New York, Las Vegas, Los Angeles, and Honolulu.

Tita Remy lived in Daly City with Uncle John Osterstock, her Scandinavian-American husband who sported an oily bald head and a glued-on grin that said he loved my aunt never mind the endless parade of relatives to which she subjected him. On our first full day, they took us on a boat tour of San Francisco Bay. We chugged beneath the Golden Gate Bridge's underbelly. The wide expanse darted in and out of fog then disappeared completely. We too were swallowed up whole. The cooling mist turned into drops of dew, seeping farther into my pores with every blast of the boat's foghorn. Lanelle and I zipped up our jackets and turned our backs to the flapping wind while the others were snug inside the windowed cabin. I noticed a man with brown wavy locks and grey-green eyes. He was dressed in a denim jacket and tan bellbottoms, sitting on a bench. He crossed his legs ankle over thigh and flashed perfect teeth at us. He must have been in his twenties or thirties.

"Look, he's smiling at you," Lanelle said as she nudged me.

I broke his piercing stare by cracking a half smile of acknowledgment before looking out for Alcatraz. The tour guide said it was to our left behind the curtain of grey.

"I bet he's gay," she said with disdain.

I continued looking for The Rock as Lanelle's words freeze-dried in my head. It was the first time I heard my sister use the word "gay." That, along with "fag," were thrown around in the hallways, locker rooms, and playing fields back in school like medicine balls. Hearing any of these words was a punch in the pit of my stomach.

I grew up hearing the Tagalog word, bakla, and had just learned the Japanese equivalent, okama, but the wavy-haired man seemed to be neither. He did not have manicured nails or lipstick like many hairdressers I saw back in the Philippines. They also wore high heels, tight jeans, and manes halfway to the floor. He reminded me of rock star Leif Garret. Goose bumps jumped onto my arms, and a steel rod shot up from spine to skull, putting me on alert.

Folks near us said it was a miracle the fog had burned off, giving way to a blast of sun. Our boat turned around and headed back to the wharf. I swallowed a lump while gazing at the towering pylon and cables that looked like giant harp strings waiting to be strummed. Leif lookalike invaded my periphery. I squeezed my eyes shut. *Go away. Go away. Please, not while my sister is here.* I opened them and turned to where he sat. He was no longer there. I did a quick 360-degree turn. He was nowhere to be found. The Golden Gate repeated its disappearing act in the distance. Even as we disembarked, I saw no sign of him. I could not peel off thoughts of being in bed with Leif lookalike, or Leif himself, both of us naked under the sheets. Whatever we were doing, it was as nebulous and captivating as the fog, now far off in the distance.

Aurora, Illinois was just over an hour's drive west of Chicago O'Hare Airport. Mommy's older sister, Tita Chit lived there with her husband Uncle Joe. Two days into our stay with them, I began to cough and felt feverish. I ended up staying in with both of them while my family drove into what they kept calling "the Windy City" for dinner with their son, my lawyer cousin, Graham, who had a loft on Lake Shore Drive overlooking Lake Michigan. I was too sick to even feel any self-pity for missing out. Tita had me take two Tylenol tablets along with tea and honey. She also had me rub Vicks VapoRub all over my chest. My eyelids turned heavy, and I dozed off to the opening credits of *Love Boat*.

In my dream were Marlboro Man, Leif Garret, and Luke Skywalker, brought to the forefront of my fantasies by our trip to Adler Planetarium on our first day. The three of them were arguing in an empty parking lot. Passersby paused and formed a circle around them. The crowd soon became a full coliseum of roaring cheers. Trumpets echoed. A full moon turned into a spotlight over them shoving at one another, just as gladiators would.

"He's with me," shouted Marlboro Man.

"You're mistaken, buster" yelled Leif.

Marlboro Man yanked his pistol out of its holster as spectators ducked for cover.

"There's only one way to settle this," declared Luke Skywalker as he brandished a blinding beam accompanied by a numbing buzz that was his Obi-Won Kenobi light saber.

I ran to the center and stretched my arms out in the hopes of averting a bloody confrontation.

"No, wait," I pleaded. "I'll decide."

The three of them fixed gazes at me as I did them. Their eyes telegraphed an undying devotion for me, but I had to pick one over the others.

"Why did we agree to go?'

Marlboro? Leif? Luke? Mommy!

"It's okay, it's over." *Tatay!*

I woke up on my side with my back to the door of the guest bedroom. The room light and TV had been turned off, but I could hear them fumble in the dark. My family had returned. But it was Tatay and Mommy who were mumbling, disgruntled over Graham having taken them and Lanelle to a gay discotheque for drinks.

"No wonder he wanted the children to stay and watch TV at his place," Mommy said.

She rested her hand against my soaking back then took a damp cold washcloth and wiped underneath my pajama top. I stretched, feigning grogginess. My cough had dissipated, and my fever had nearly disappeared, though my nerves were frayed. I prayed for the stiffness between my legs to subside. I tried to picture Brooke Shields in her denim commercial, but it was not helping either. I cupped my erection and quietly asked Marlboro Man, Leif Garrett, and Luke Skywalker to reconvene. But alas, that channel had turned to static, the end of programming, and all I was left with was a wish that all three of my heartthrobs would always love me and never leave me.

"Good night, good boy," Mommy whispered.

New York, New York. My eyes strained to take in midday Manhattan as our Checker cab raced from La Guardia Airport toward the 59th Street Bridge.

Tatay sat next to the driver, pointing out landmarks whose silhouettes had been branded in my psyche long before they stood before me now: the World Trade Twin Towers, the Chrysler Building, Rockefeller Center, United Nations, and the Empire State Building. But for every recognizable structure in my snow globe view of the city, there were hundreds of others I wanted to enter, to know better. Four days was not going to be enough. I was already sure I would have to return to the island of Manhattan even before I stepped foot on it.

"First time in the city?" yelled the jovial Black driver over his shoulder. Rossana and Jonas were on fold-down chairs facing Mommy, Lanelle, and me, all of us squeezed in the back seat with our hand carry. The trunk, tied down with rope over six pieces of luggage, flapped whenever the cab hit a bump.

"You be sure to stick close by your parents, you hear me now? It's easy to get lost in the Big Apple." He must have read my mind as I tried to figure out how I was going to explore the city on my own without a map or chaperone.

Tatay's older brother, Tito Teddy, lived on his own on the Upper East Side. My cousins Veda and Mary Lee were in the Upper East Side as well, one married, the other engaged. I noted my ties to the city for future reference. Having relatives in Manhattan also meant there was no time to waste as we were shuttled to all the must-sees: the Metropolitan Museum, MOMA, Wall Street, Chinatown, the Statue of Liberty, Central Park, and Times Square. A whirlwind-within-a-whirlwind tour. Sometimes we were divvied up to make catching taxis more manageable so we could cover more ground. Each night Lanelle, Rossana, Jonas and I played a game of "guess what I saw today." I even got to take a side trip on the Metro-North to Connecticut with Tito to visit artist friends of his and to have dinner with a restaurant critic for *The New York Times*.

Then there was Broadway. I was entranced by the clever movements of the Mummenschanz dance troupe. My first ever Broadway musical was *Annie*, starring Sarah Jessica Parker. The following night, I cupped my face with my palm away from my parents and Lanelle as tears dripped onto my playbill in the mezzanine level of the Shubert Theater where the cast of *A Chorus Line* belted out what they did for love, just as I had done in the ensemble of Showtime '79 back in Tokyo. As we left the theater, Lanelle asked if I had noticed the gay character that looked like the guy we saw on the boat.

"Huh?" I shrugged my shoulders. *I love New York.*

On our fourth and final morning, as we were about to order breakfast at the coffee shop of the Doral Inn where we were staying, Mommy walked in and headed toward Tatay, Lanelle, and me.

"Are Rossana and Jonas here?" she asked in a frantic falsetto.

"Where are they?" Tatay said.

"They said they were coming down here."

We all jumped out of our booth and darted into the lobby. We asked the doorman if he had seen two kids walk out, but he said he was just starting his shift. Tatay barked orders for Mommy and Lanelle to head north on Lexington Avenue while he went south.

"What about me?" I said. "I can go west."

"Wait in the room," he said as Mommy pressed the room key into my palm. "If they show up, keep them there until we return."

We had less than two hours before checkout at noon and our ride to the airport. As the three of them ran out the revolving door, I headed toward the bank of gold elevators. The next available car was five floors above and falling at a snail's pace.

I was envious, actually downright angry my sister and brother had managed to escape. When they joined forces, I was no match for their nerve and verve. They had never let me in on their secrets and adventures since the day I tricked them into eating hot peppers off a plant I said was a candy tree.

I wanted time to myself in the city. But scare tactics like murder, kidnapping, and subway muggings were used to keep children tethered to an adult family member at all times. I felt adult enough to explore on my own, but I also fretted over wandering off and having to fabricate some story to justify my whereabouts no matter how benign the truth may have been. Why did I always assume guilt for wanting to be by myself?

A small group of Japanese tourists, five senior citizens, all with JTB (Japan Travel Bureau) pins on their lapels gabbed like hens in a coop while we waited for the elevator. I eavesdropped on their conversation about the clear and cool for July morning outside. Even this far away from home, they did not cease talking about the weather—their default for avoiding uncomfortable silences and perhaps to even dodge any real conversation. As they compared room numbers, I wondered whether the JAL campaign with Circus's song swayed them into signing up for their package tour.

The elevator pinged open. Many guests with suitcases, filed out. The last to exit was a man with auburn curls and black rimmed glasses framing hamster pink eyes. He looked right at me before heading for the lobby.

I let the tour group file past me so I could watch him. He stopped in mid-step, then turned around and retraced his steps, as if he had forgotten something upstairs. I turned away.

"Please, after you," he said. His brows spoke louder than his voice.

We got in with the tour group, and I pressed the eighth floor. He hit the seven button even though it was already lit. As the doors closed, I turned to my left to get a better look at him: weak jaw, bent nose, hairs sprouting from his ear. He was by no means an ad icon, rock star, or movie hero. The elevator car lacked circulation, stuffy with aftershave, potent perfume, and halitosis.

The tour group emptied out onto the seventh floor. He kept his finger on the "door open" button long enough for me to notice and for him to figure out his next move. I could not help but shake my head. It was a game of musical floors, like back at the Imperial Hotel. I then took a chess-like step back against the backside of the car. He released the button, slowly stepped out, and turned to lock eyes with me once more as if to say checkmate. The doors closed on him.

Eighth floor. I immediately pressed the seventh floor button. I felt for my Adam's apple, averting my eyes from the security camera as the elevator crawled back down to seven. My temples throbbed. I held on to the guardrail. The elevator steadied itself before reopening. I stepped out and turned left. A ray of sunlight fell across the carpeting halfway down the hall, emanating from a partially open door.

I exhaled through my mouth, tension thrusting into thin air. I took timid steps toward the solar finish line, overcome with déjà vu.

I knocked, peered in, and closed the door behind me.

"We need to make this quick. I've got people waiting," he said in a raspy voice, devoid of any formalities or salutations. He was already unbuttoning his white short-sleeve polyester shirt, loosening his diagonally striped blue tie, and undoing his belt buckle.

I unbuckled my belt, too. He walked right up to me and clumsily unzipped my Levi's. Then he knelt down before me and attended to my Jockey-clad crotch with his teeth. It was halfway between a gnaw and a caress. I was at attention in no time, and my briefs turned moist. By him or me or both, I was not sure.

"I really am out of time," he said, more to himself than to me.

Nonetheless, I nodded. His cock erect, he remained standing while he masturbated, as if against the clock. I did the same. We were mirror images trying to finish off what we had started. It was not how I envisioned my first sexual encounter, at least the first I'd entered fully aware, able and willing. And that I tried to bring to some mutually satisfying conclusion. It hardly held a candle to the fantasies and dreams I had woven so intricately throughout this trip. What this stranger and I were left with was a mechanical, chemical, and hormonal, if not downright carnal, act, without an emotional spark to our shaking fists, facial twists, and forced moans.

We seemed to be wire-fused as he grabbed on to my shoulder, bending our knees and grunting as we simultaneously shot diagonally away from each other onto the cream carpet floor. Liquid fire flowed out of me, the whole trip's worth, as meteors showered inside my head. In a flash, I imagined Marlboro Man, Leif Garrett, and Luke Skywalker staring at me from across the room. Disgust and dejection was etched in their eyes. They turned their backs and exited the room.

"Forget the mess," he said as he frantically pulled up his pants.

I zipped up and briskly hand-ironed my prized turquoise Lacoste knit shirt as I tucked it into my jeans before running out of the room and down the hallway.

Marlboro! Leif! Luke! Wait for me, I wanted to cry out. *Please don't leave me.*

I thought they had scurried into the closing elevator. I tried to pry open the door but was unable to do so. I caught a glimpse of their tear-stained faces. Luke seemed to mouth, *We'll always love you. Goodbye, Jobert.*

Man! Leif! Luke! I screamed to myself as their car ascended to the twenty-eighth and top floor.

I waited for the next elevator to take me up after them. When I bolted out, all I saw was a Hispanic cleaning lady and her rolling workstation. "Housekeeping," she said as she knocked on doors. *Excuse me, but have you seen a cowboy, rock star and space hero walk by?* I retreated into the elevator, my head toward the floor as if an anvil had been slung across my sternum.

Back in my room, I ran into the bathroom, removed all my clothes, and jumped into the shower. I couldn't control my sobs. I was unable to rinse off the film of filth. Nor was I able to wash my brain from what just happened, let alone this diseased desire of wanting to play with men's cocks that felt more right than wrong. A longing and loneliness gnawed at me. I swatted my arms, then my chest. I pounded my head with both of my palms, determined to punish myself.

I was a bad Catholic for sinning on something I couldn't bring myself to say penance for even if the priest was unable to identify me through the confessional screen.

I was an utter disappointment to my parents. They would never approve, and I would be banished from...well, I had no idea, though the consequence was to be direr than when my mother accused my father of having an affair.

I was a filthy boy. I was turning into something unrecognizable, if not diabolic, for having these yearnings society didn't tolerate. Which explained why men furtively roamed the world, transmitting codes to others who were on the same wavelength. And in hotels, whether it be in Tokyo, Kyoto, or New York. And I imagined everywhere else.

I hurt myself until I turned red. Until it felt futile to do so. This new skin or whatever it was that drove me to want what was forbidden, would stick to me and be part of who I was here on out.

Fearful my family would return at any moment, I wiped away my tears as the shower's stream was still splashing on my face. I somehow snapped out of my spiral to put on a 'clean kitchen' act. I dried myself in haste before running over to look out the window.

Below was Lexington Avenue where ant people were moving at various velocities in different directions, including my family, all five of them. I could make them out as they walked hand-in-hand back into the hotel. Rossana and Jonas would later say they made a side trip to Bloomingdale's farther up Lexington Avenue. They would not suffer any consequence for their actions beyond, "you almost gave us a heart attack."

If anything, their trip will have been a resounding success symbolized by the oversized stuffed elephant they won at Six Flags Great Adventure, waiting for them back at Tita Remy's in California. Tatay would happily pay for the excess baggage as we returned to Tokyo.

I, on the other hand, did not have any such memento to show for on this American adventure. If anything I lost Leif, Luke, and Marlboro Man for good on this trip. They were no longer sufficient fantasies to quench my raging libido. As confusing as it all seemed, what I undeniably wanted was to be naked with a man. To feel his flesh and he mine. To smell and taste him, whoever he might happen to be. I didn't need to know his name or anything much about him after all.

Could such a hunger within be devoid of love and romance that lived in the song lyrics I cherished? Perhaps so, I thought as I plunged headfirst into unchartered waters.

I hugged myself tight, as if to stabilize myself into this new realm of reality. I looked up at the slice of cobalt blue sky high above the honking taxis, that urban symphony, the canon of concrete, the colony of humanity, on this island of Manhattan, in the city of New York, in the Empire State of New York, in these United States of America.

14
Political Theater

Tokyo, 1979

"So, who do you think will run?" asked Helmut, looking at both Seung Poon and me. "It's your turn this year, Jobert."

Helmut wiggled bushy brows over almond eyes, thanks to his German mother and Japanese father. We were seated on a café au lait colored couch in the Guidance Center, a narrow lounge that separated Mr. Hauet's office from the hallway. A week into tenth grade, we gathered here to gab, something we had dared not do as freshmen. It was our lunch period, and most of our classmates were outdoors on the basketball courts and courtyard, soaking up September's waning warmth.

"Yes, that makes sense," said John, who was Japanese but American by birth.

Seung Poon and Han Jun nodded in unison. Both had Korean roots, though they'd spent their entire lives in Japan. I had overheard somewhere the Japanese looked down on Koreans, and that the Koreans, in return, despised the Japanese, perhaps not unlike how my relatives felt, given imperial aggression during World War II and denial over atrocities committed, like using thousands of "comfort women" for Japanese soldiers throughout the region. The notion of forced sex frightened and excited me. I was mum on the subject of racial prejudice, which I did not detect, at least outwardly, in school, as well as the fact that the Japanese executed my grandparents and tortured my father's family.

I, too, nodded while stifling a smile. I stared at shelves full of yearbooks, SAT and TOEFL test prep guides, and college catalogues organized by both country and state that lined the length of the room. Unlike the juniors and seniors walking in and out of Mr. Hauet's office, thoughts of college and high school graduation were galaxies away for any of us, despite Mr. Hauet's insistence the day before in Careers class that we were to start asking ourselves where we might want to apply.

I had been hoping they would support my candidacy. Yes, I wanted to be class president. Seung Poon had won the year before, boosted by his brother, who then was Student Council president. They both did decent jobs, but it was my turn. I had worked hard at forging friendships and acquiring acquaintances since eighth grade, and my overall reputation remained intact. I was pretty sure no one suspected me of being gay even though the thought of acknowledging it to myself so confidently felt dangerous and headily exhilarating. At least I was not associated with the one or two question marks in high school, who liked to watch black-and-white films starring the likes of Bette Davis and discuss them incessantly at lunchtime.

Becoming class president would distract me from my wanton thoughts. More importantly, it would deflect any suspicion others might have had. No one would have thought the class president a fag. Would they?

My mind was on overdrive. Having just returned from my family's US vacation, I was wise to hotels as hangouts for homosexuals and felt foolish to have had yet another hasty, unsatisfactory sexual encounter with an unsavory type. The scene at the Doral Inn remained vivid and dizzyingly potent, like the scent of a fresh coat of enamel.

Since New York, sex and my mental renderings of it had taken permanent refuge inside my head. Every few minutes, a carnal image flicked by at the pace of flipping through a stack of snapshots. I caught glimpses of porn scenes on nightly adult TV shows after 11 p.m.; Tom of Finland S&M paperback covers displayed in a revolving metal rack on the second floor of the *Kinokuniya* bookstore in the Ginza shopping district; the hirsute American basketball and wrestling coaches at St. Mary's who paraded in bulging jockstraps in their own locker room office next to the showers. I had no control over the order or frequency of these visuals, these snippets of mental video, though I found myself masturbating early in the morning in addition to late at night, coming twice, thrice, or more times a day, until my dick was chafed. In school, though, I was extra careful to conceal my hodgepodge of horniness underneath an armor of normality.

Helmut, John, Seung Poon, and Han Jun comprised half of the eight or so students who had attended St. Mary's since first grade, out of a class of sixty. They could have certainly influenced the Asian vote, the largest voting block made up mostly of Japanese, Koreans, and hafus. I called all four of them friends and hung out with them more than anyone else. None of them turned me on sexually, and I grimaced when such a scenario strayed through my head. Assuming I was the only Asian running for president, my chances seemed pretty good.

I also maintained ties to the Westerners. There were a handful of Africans and Europeans, both Western and Eastern. Two had fathers working at the United Nations University as well, so I counted them into my imaginary plus column, and I was friendly with the Australians. They could put me over the top, unless one of them entered the race.

The final constituency to consider was the Americans, the wild cards, given their varying degrees of assimilation and association with the Asians and Europeans. If one of the Americans ran, then my calculations may not have added up. I was fully aware of the power they wielded. Many in school seemed to kowtow unknowingly to them.

On Election Day, the two sophomore homerooms came together. Nominations were made, speeches given, votes cast, and the results tallied in a matter of minutes.

Throughout the process, I saw Helmut and Han Jun pass notes to the other Asians in the room. Although there were several nominations, most withdrew. Richard, an Australian, was the only other contender, and I won by a margin of three to one.

Some shouted, "speech, speech" while others applauded and whistled. *Wow, they really like me.*

I stood up, basked in the adulation, and thanked everyone profusely.

"Class of '82 will be the best class St. Mary's has ever had," I said. "We'll have a cool school dance and class trip, and I'll represent your interests at all Student Council meetings." Then I bowed and threw my arms up in a banzai stance, something a corrupt politician might do.

After all, politics was theater. And knowing my way around the school stage was how I was going to survive, to stay in character as straight while within the confines of St. Mary's International School.

"Mommy, guess what? I won the class election." I shouted into the phone as if she was in another country.

"Oh, that's great, Jobert. I'll tell your father at work right away." Hearing this, I held off from relaying any more details.

"Some of us are going out for curry to celebrate, okay? I'll be home by seven."

As I put the receiver down in Mr. Hauet's office, I looked out his window onto the basketball court before puffing up my chest and returning to my natural slouch. *I've made my parents proud again.*

Seung Poon and Han Jun had cross country practice after school. I was better suited for sprints, and hence decided not to run. Besides, I had to make my mark as class president. This left Helmut, John, and me to head to a Japanese curry house at the bottom of the hill for cube-shaped cuts of potato and pork drenched in sweet, steaming sauce the color of mud, in a large bowl of rice. I added a chunk of pickled radish, bleeding with red dye. It became one of my favorite Japanese dishes.

"Well, the elections turned out as expected," said Helmut.

"Thanks again," I said. "Now the real work starts."

"You'll do well," said John.

"You'll do fine," said Helmut. "You won't let us down."

We were done by four thirty, and the three of us parted ways at the train station. I was only half-aware that my steps veered away from the platform for the train home on the Toyoku Line. I switched to the Hibiya subway line instead. I was on autopilot in the opposite direction.

The doors chimed before closing. I sat down, wantonly caressing the maroon velvet upholstery. Maybe five, ten, even fifteen minutes later, more sexual images shot by in rapid succession before me. I could not keep up. They seemed to scatter all over the floor. I jerked out of my hallucination into attention, gathering my thoughts into some semblance of order.

I can't believe I'm doing this.

I looked around to see if anyone had seen me panic. No one in the half-empty car paid me any attention. The metal wheels squealed in ecstasy as the subway rollicked through the pitch-black tunnel toward the center of Tokyo, and on to my ultimate destination: The Imperial Hotel.

I had not been back inside the hotel since spring. Renovation was underway on a wing of rooms to be connected to the main structure, which housed the arcade and lobby. As I walked by a "Please pardon our appearance" placard in the lobby, I realized I was still in my school uniform. I undid my blue knit tie and shoved it inside my backpack. Then I unbuttoned the top of my white, long-sleeve shirt, allowing the crescent collar of my white, cotton T-shirt to show through. Finally, I removed my blazer and held it as a waiter would a serving cloth, folded on one arm, careful to conceal the St. Mary's insignia.

The underground shopping arcade was a Tower of Babel, overflowing with guests speaking Italian, French, Spanish, Hebrew, English, and two or more languages I did not recognize. One of them I was guessing to be Greek. I wove through the corridor's labyrinth of limbs and shopping bags, and I looped the arcade twice, figuring no one would mind me. All the stores were as I remembered them, with the exception of the one with the mural screen display. Once a spring tea ceremony, it had transformed into a fiery autumnal forest with a Shinto shrine tori gate in the foreground and storks flying past the silhouette of Mount Fuji.

I am class president. I wanted to do more than eat curry in celebration. I did not feel like buying another single or album. Nor did I want to play Space Invaders or Pac-Man in a game center. I wanted to make those images inside my head come to life. I wanted to find someone. Seduce them. And get naked.

I circled the arcade a fourth time, blankly staring into more displays yet alert to any darting eyes or over-friendly smiles. There were none to be found. I began to wonder what had happened to all the men who seemed to be cruising up a storm in the spring?

I spied a man on his own on the other end of the walkway. He had a nest of light brown curls perched over wind-burned cheeks. His thin black rimmed glasses were halfway down his nose in grandma fashion as he sifted through painted paper wallets in a bin by the door of a souvenir shop. He was in a short-sleeve batik print shirt with loud swirls and triangles of mustard and purple, offset by a thick gold chain, resting on his clavicle. He reminded me of Gene Wilder in Woody Allen's, *Everything You Always Wanted to Know About Sex*, which I had watched on my own in a movie theater one afternoon after school.

I stood on the other side of the door pretending to check the price of a daruma, a papier-mâché doll dressed in a red robe, whose left eye was painted in when making a resolution, and right eye when the challenge was successful. Unlike Japanese politicians who colored one eye as they kicked off their campaigns, I was eager to color in both eyes at once with today's victory.

Look here, over here.

He did, heeding my suggestive powers. He then looked down and back up again. He was staring at me if not right through me. I wanted to turn around and see what he saw behind me. He barely cracked a smile before returning his attention to the wallets.

I remained rooted to the floor and was still staring at him. I caught a whiff of Paco Rabanne.

"That's Paco Rabanne," I said.

"Excuse me?"

"Paco Rabanne. I was trying to identify the cologne you are wearing." *Jobert, shit, control yourself.*

"Actually, it's Pierre Cardin. Though I do wear Paco now and then." His accent was as if his words were halfway down his throat.

"I'm sorry, I didn't mean to bother you." *Yes I did.*

His fingers froze among the wallets. "You know your colognes, you cheeky thing you."

I giggled, not sure what "cheeky" meant, then caught myself doing so. "Not really..." I couldn't think of a comeback.

He pulled up a wallet. "What do you think of this?"

It was a painting of a warrior carrying a bow and sword behind his back. He was seated next to a man composing a letter, perhaps poetry. "It'll make a great gift, I'm sure."

"Yeah, I think you're right, mate." I wanted him to slow down so I could catch everything he said. *Where's he from?* "Cheers."

I took this as my signal to scoot. "Bye."

"Wait," he said. "I just want to pay for these. Would you like to have coffee?"

"I don't drink coffee but maybe..."

"Just wait right there." He picked up a handful of wallets and paid for them inside. I took a few steps down the corridor and looked into the tea store. *I suppose he's okay.* I checked the time: 6:00.

He caught up with me and extended his hand over my shoulder. "Hi, I'm Stan."

Definitely Paco Rabanne. I turned toward him. "Hi, I'm Joseph. Call me Joe."

"How old are you, Joe?"

Fif—"Ah, sixteen, almost seventeen."

"You look mature for seventeen. Care to walk?"

"Where to?"

"Well, how 'bout my room?" His words rang out like three sevens on a slot machine.

"Uh..." I looked back at my watch.

"I'll cut to the chase, mate. How's 5,000 yen?"

What?

"Room 302, In five minutes."

15

The New Zealander

Tokyo, 1979

"That feels so good," I said, halfway between a whimper and a whisper. My eyes were shut, and my mind wandered into an Eden of ecstasy. Stan's fingers kneaded out the knobs in my shoulder and neck. It was bliss and torture all at once.

"How's that?" he asked as his fingertips crawled toward my temples like a drunk tarantula. "Much better?'

I looked up from where I was seated, in front of a mahogany desk with a touch-tone phone, a banker's lamp, and a burgundy, leather bound folder that read "Information & Room Service" in scratched-up gold lettering. I looked over my right shoulder and nodded at him, even though I could not see him. "Mm, much, much better, yes."

I had not read *The Japan Times* and Jeane Dixon's astrological forecast, though I did make a note to review it in relation to my day's highlights. First, being elected class president, then designated captain of the sophomore Brain Bowl team, and finally, at the Imperial Hotel, gaining a new appreciation for massage, sessions Mommy claimed did wonders for the circulation and psyche. Oh, and there was the money, 5,000 yen, five weeks' allowance that I intended to leave with this time.

My chest galloped, picking up speed as Stan mimicked chopping motions up and down my back with his hands cupped into a clam. The resulting sounds reminded me of Pac-Man earning points as he gobbled polka dots along his path.

His index fingers rappelled from my forehead down to my cheeks onto my throat. *What if he chokes me?* They then landed on my torso where they swirled over the cotton fabric veiling my chest. My nipples jutted out at attention. A shiver shot down my legs. I let out a moan, somewhat for effect.

"Come here," he said.

I followed him to the base of the king-size bed wrapped in a bedspread of forest green, not a crumb or crease to spoil its deceptive perfection.

I took a deep breath. "Before we go any further…"

"Before we go any further," he echoed. He smiled and pulled from his back pocket a wallet of shiny cordovan snakeskin. "Here you go, you cheeky bastard." There was no harshness in his voice, but his native brogue worsened as he counted out the bills.

"One…two…three…four…and five." He handed them to me one over the other, like a payout on some cheesy daytime game show.

"Thank you."

I took the crisp cash to a corner of the room and rolled it up like a doobie before zipping it in my knapsack which I had left on the celery-colored couch by the curtained window. This was a watershed moment.

The monetary transaction seemed easy enough. It was downright exhilarating. And if I was able to pull this off, perhaps I could do it with others as well. After all, I was offering a service by taking off my clothes as they did the same, even if there might be a questionable aspect to it.

I vaguely recalled a friend of my parents joke that prostitution was the world's oldest profession. I didn't think it applied to me as this was a one-off occurrence. But then I realized I had been relying on my weekly allowance as my only source of income, and unlike my more Japanese-fluent classmates, I was unable to get a part-time job or arubaito—アルバイト—a sort of badge of honor among them, which meant more money to spend at Game Centers and on ramen or yakisoba snacks. They were mostly busboys and English teachers to Japanese kids. I believed I had found my own arubaito, albeit an unconventional one that paid a lot more by the hour with the caveat that I could not share this fact.

I turned toward him. "So, where were we?" I was taken aback by the cheap singsong seduction of my own words.

He reached for my shirt buttons and plucked on them as if he was expecting them to reverberate into melodious chords. I prayed he didn't unthread let alone break any of them. *But Mommy, it just fell off.*

"Such smooth skin," he said, gliding the back of his hand over my cheek and under my chin. "When did you shave last?"

Does he mean with a razor? "Oh, last week."

"Nice." He placed too much emphasis at the end, sounding like a feline's hiss.

That was close. I had yet to start shaving, really. Some of the boys in class already did, mostly the Americans and Europeans. I could tell because one day they would have stubbled faces that turned spotless overnight with maybe a nick or two to show for it, the scars of becoming a man. This seemed less so among Asians. I thought we were inferior in this regard. No one ever talked about shaving.

Stan returned to my buttons. He first released the top then moved intently to the one below and so forth until all six were undone. He concentrated on the task at hand, never looking into my eyes. I was preoccupied with my dick, which was about to betray me as it swelled under my flannel slacks. *Play it cool. Don't be desperate.* Sweat trickled down his forehead onto my shirt. I wanted to run and wash it off for fear it would stain. *Mommy, curry must have splattered.* I was about to sneeze to fresh squirts of Pierre Cardin, still Paco Rabanne to me.

"You're shivering," he said.

"It's a little cold in here, that's all."

"I'll take care of that." He removed my shirt from my goose bumped arms and laid it over the desk chair. He then rubbed his hands against one another as if in an effort to ignite a fire. He blew into the cavity of his cupped hands and laid them over my arms, then my elbows, and finally, my hands. His eyes closed in meditation, he seemed determined to heal me of my maladies.

"You're one fine specimen," he said.

Should I say, 'thank you'? Perhaps it was best to be silent and await his next move.

My waist, all twenty-six inches of it, contracted after he unbuckled my belt and slithered it out of its loops. He toyed with the waistband of my briefs along my hips down to my ass, which he patted twice.

"Mm...nice and firm."

He unzipped my trousers and held them by the pockets so I could step out. I grasped his shoulder for balance. Stan's tongue, the color and texture of sliced Spam, circled his lips, leaving a glossy finish. He pulled down my briefs. I was fully erect.

For the next minute, I was not myself. I must have left my body and floated into midair. Was this what they meant by achieving nirvana? Even if ever so fleetingly? Never before had I experienced the sensation of my dick slipping in and out of someone's mouth. I was on the verge of passing out.

Instead, I ejaculated with little warning. Its intensity sputtered up my spine. I felt a squeeze at the base and heard sucking sounds, squealing with every spasm, my legs and arms flailing like Linda Blair in *The Exorcist*.

Spent, I pinched my eyes shut before reaching down to the head of my dick, panicked that I had failed to contain the mess. Stan emerged, smiling, before falling back on his back and to my side. I was eye level with his Adam's apple, rhythmically swaying as he swallowed. He uttered smacking noises, reapplying saliva to his lips.

And it is I who is getting paid for this.

The woman behind the reception desk frowned as she clacked again at a keyboard behind the icy marble counter. "Sorry, sir. I check one more time. No one by the name Banssu."

"That can't be," I said. "He's supposed to have arrived yesterday. Barnes. B-A-R-N-E-S."

"Let me find out in office."

She turned around and pushed her way through a door camouflaged by the wall's dark licorice exterior. She twisted her neck to catch a good glimpse of me before she disappeared inside. I returned a clipped smile. *Hurry up.*

It had been two weeks since Stan knotted his eager arms around my back and planted baby's breath kisses all over my cheeks, chest, and thighs. Two weeks since he made me come twice in half an hour, once in his mouth and again with his hands, leaving me in a swoon with a gooey mess on my chest. Two weeks since he told me he was a barrister from Auckland on holiday, and that he would return to Tokyo and the Imperial Hotel after skiing in Sapporo. He wanted us to "hook up again for more fun," his exact words as we parted. I agreed to a rendezvous. He guaranteed I would make double what I did the first time.

Did I properly remember his surname? The woman returned with a colleague in standard Japanese sa-ra-ri-man attire: a dark blue polyester-wool suit, matching tie, white dress shirt, and a company pin branded onto his jacket lapel—in this case, what looked like a gold chrysanthemum, the Imperial Seal of Japan. He was at least twice as tall and old as she was, with an air of seniority about him.

"Who you rookin preesu?" he asked. For a second, I was taken aback by his heavy Tokyo accent, given the international environment in which he supposedly functioned.

"I am to meet a family friend here today. Mr. Stan Barnes." I exaggerated my accent. I didn't know what I was going for, though I feigned a brogue not unlike Stan's.

"We chekku but no anyone with name Bansu-san." He and the woman looked back at me with cardboard faces.

"But he was here two weeks ago. In room 302. Please check your records." I heard the man mutter, "hidoi," which I understood to mean "awful." Head down, he was now clacking away too fast for any keyboard to keep up.

Who are you calling awful? Me, because you can read right through my façade, and decipher my motives? Me, because you've seen this scenario one too many times before? Me, because I dare challenge your policy on guest privacy? Me, because I have the gall to pursue such nonsense? Fuck, maybe Stan really isn't Stan Barnes, and I've been had. Fuck, he wouldn't do that, would he? No. Yes. I can't believe this. Maybe he's been delayed. Maybe he had to cancel. Fuck, I'm too intelligent and street smart to be taken for a ride. I'm no fool. Stay calm. Just walk away.

"Thank you." I immediately turned around and headed toward the stairwell to the arcade below. I could feel the weight of their stares on my back urging me to keep moving. *Stay cool. Screw them. Don't look back.*

I speed-walked with no particular destination in mind. I first took a right at the bottom of the stairs through one wing of the arcade toward the subway entrance. I then walked up an exit that poured out onto a sidewalk, along the impenetrable, slanting granite walls of the Imperial Palace grounds, cordoned off by a murky moat. I played back what had just happened, first from my perspective and then theirs before I dug deeper to two weeks ago, searching for the one dead giveaway to prove that Stan had been out to deceive me after all.

Does anyone even ski in Sapporo in late September? Shit! This is retribution for being greedy. For being a liar. God is getting back at me for lying to Mommy about spending time with my friends. This fucking stinks.

I carried on with myself for several minutes. It was too easy to do, and no one was the wiser. The histrionic me at my best, or worst as the case may be, wallowed in self-pity, my thoughts calling out for attention like television reporters yelling questions and shoving microphones at the indicted emerging from a courthouse. I was Pontius Pilate, Jesus Christ and angry mob chorus all at once:

Did you actually take money in exchange for sex?

Yes, I did.

Guilty.

Did you really think he would return?

Yes, I did.

Burn.

Who's the fool?

I am. I don't care. I'd do it again. Take me away. Woe is me.

Crucify him.

What have you got to say for yourself?

I'll get you for this, Stan Barnes, or whatever the fuck your name is. No one screws with me.

Ha-ha-ha-ha!

I retraced my steps all the way back into the arcade. Just as I had gravitated here in celebration when I became class president, I did so again, only now with rage and wanting to seek some kind of revenge. It did not matter who I would take out my anger on. I wanted to have sex, damn it. That was, after all, what I had come here for in the first place.

Oh, and for the money as well.

16

The Italian

Stan Barnes. Son of a bitch.

Upon turning the corner where the haberdashery bumped up against the beauty salon, I collided with a man whose response was to grab me by my upper arms. Startled, I yelped and said, "Excuse me," as he came into focus.

"Mi scusi." His tobacco-stained smile lit up under lush, black curls and a handlebar mustache that was as shiny as a brand new bicycle. I guessed him to be forty something.

"I'm so, so, sorry."

"It is no problem," he said, releasing his grip on me. We both remained motionless.

He was draped in some kind of shawl. I had never seen pants with so many pleats, not unlike velvet curtains on a theater stage. He was in toffee colored leather sandals, his toenails thick as half-moons. It was all a bit too summery for early October, and dramatic for any time of year. He was not the type I would be drawn to instantly, but there was something enigmatic, if not magnetic, about his entire ensemble, something very *Arabian Nights* even though it was all so krook-krook—my family's made-up term for something gaudy and ghastly.

"Hello, hello," he said, fluttering a hand in front of me, as if to bring me out of hypnosis. "Do you know what time it is?" I had heard Filipino waiters feigning his accent before at the Italian Village in Manila, taking pizza and pasta orders.

I looked at my Seiko, then at his Bulova before I looked back at him. "Four. A good time." I winked, then rubbed my eye as if to take back what I had unexpectedly, even unintentionally, put out there.

"I see. I see. You are alone?"

"Of course." *Start at 5,000 yen.*

"And what are you selling, I mean shopping?" He too winked. *This is way too easy.*

"What are you offering?"

"I'm ordering room service. Vino too. Will you join me?"

Food? I can eat something. "Sure, why not?"

"Let us go then."

"No wait." I turned to look around. *Shit, someone from the front desk might see me.* "Just tell me your room number."

"Room 2020."

"Perfect."

"You will come now?"

"Yes, yes." I shooed him off with my hands and walked away without looking back, then I turned another corner.

"So, you are from where?"

"Manila."

"Ah, yes, I guessed so."

Oh, did you? Shit. I always wanted to keep them guessing. "And you? Rome?"

"Milano."

"Vacation?"

"Business. I am on my way to Manila."

Hmm. Flowing garb. "You are a fashion designer?"

He guffawed then took a sip from the grossly overpriced chianti he had just uncorked from the minibar. I knew because I saw the price, 16,500 yen, as I walked into the bathroom to soap my hands, splash my face, squeeze a neck pimple, and straighten my posture. I had returned to my chair, diagonal to his, the window to our back throwing what I had learned in geometry class to be a parallelogram of daylight across the jade carpet and tangent to the edge of the bed. We were separated by a round coffee table, empty except for an ashtray, a slender blue and white vase with a single rose, its thorns glistening and stem arching toward me, and the open bottle of wine.

"I am a talent scout. I look for actors for musicals. You Filipinos are so musical. Fabulous singers, excellent dancers."

Pride prickled through me. "It must be our Latin and Hollywood roots."

He chuckled. "And can you sing and dance?"

"Yes, but I have other talents as well." I cocked my head to the left and smiled. Nice segue if I did say so myself.

"You will audition these talents for me." He lasciviously uncrossed his legs and moved them back and forth like garden clippers before sinking into his chair and resting his wineglass at an angle over his crotch.

As if on cue, I stood up and walked toward him. He was rubbing what I gathered was a growing bulge while gulping down more wine. I craved some background music. Something that drowned the silence of the room. Something to put me in the mood. Something to perform by for Mr. Talent Scout over here. I downed my own glass of wine and winced. I did not know yet how to savor it.

I am on a makeshift stage. Strobe lights blink and mirror balls spin by to Gloria Gaynor's "I Will Survive." I can barely see the silhouettes of my enthralled audience, seated at tables with votive candles, surrounded by an aura of purple cigarette smoke. I teasingly disrobe: first my shirt, then my undershirt, then my pants, gyrating my hips at all times. I cringed at my fantasy just as I was about to pull down my briefs.

"Wait one minute," he said, raising his index finger. He got up from his seat and headed for the bathroom. "I'll be right back."

He left the door ajar. I heard the stream of urine against toilet water, followed by a flush and a running faucet. I returned to my seat still in my underwear, my boner sculpted into a circus tent, my hands clasped in a feeble attempt to disguise my giddiness.

He returned in a plush, white terrycloth robe. Barefoot, he raised his arms and smiled, as if to say, "ta-dah," and was about to commence a performance of his own. He untied the belt that held his robe taut around his waist and let it drop to the floor.

Holy Shit.

I clutched the arms of my chair as if I had just hit turbulence. I gawked at his dick. Words failed me. It must have been as long as a ruler, maybe longer. It did not look real dangling like one of Tarzan's vines. I was spectator to a freak show.

"Wow...that's very big."

"You like it?' He stroked it then swung it like a lasso.

Silence.

Does it even work? "How does it feel?"

"Fine. Many men don't like it. They say it hurts." I didn't fully process what he meant. "Come and touch it. Don't be afraid."

I tentatively walked up, my head trembling. I was transported back to six years ago, when my family visited the Taj Mahal in Agra. Tatay had paid a wad of rupees for a snake charmer to entertain us. I wanted to prove to my family I was not afraid to touch the python resting like a boa around both Rossana's Jonas's necks. As I reached out, the charmer grabbed my leg, jokingly I was later told. I screamed and cried all the way back to the Oberoi Hotel, much to everyone's amusement. *How dare they laugh at me.*

The serpent before me felt flaccid and scaly, like an uncooked spring roll. I petted it with my index fingers as if to signal I was not going to hurt it, therefore it in turn was not going to harm me. I was less aroused than fascinated.

"Would you like to suck it?"

You mean as in Stan sucking my dick, suck? "Uh...it's so big."

"Big is good. Go ahead."

I stared at his cock, which he continued stroking lovingly. I did a quick calculation of where this act stood in relation to the other one with Stan. I was not quite sure what price to quote.

"Two thousand yen," I blurted out.

"*Ecusi?*"

"I'll suck you for two thousand yen."

His body recoiled as if to say, you have got to be kidding. My eyes never left his. He looked down at his dick then back at me. "Okay, okay. Two thousand yen."

"I'll take the money first."

He jerked his head up at the ceiling and invoked some saint's name, or more likely, swore to high heaven.

"You Filipinos are also very good business people. How you say it? Enterprising."

He disappeared into the bathroom again, then emerged with two thousand yen bills crumpled in his fist. He tossed them me.

"Two thousand yen. Just suck me," he said. "Do it now."

I knelt before him. It was the first time I had done so for something other than Mass, confession, or holy communion. A pang of sacrilege gnawed from within. *It's only flesh.* My heart sprinted, though my erection had lost its firmness, falling to half-mast. I almost did not care whether I was here or not. In fact, part of me had already checked out from this episode, leaving the rest of me still present to fulfill my end of the bargain. His dick was now at eye level and up close. I was on the verge of bursting out in laughter. *It is quite ugly.* Why did the thought or mention of penis, dick, cock, prick, schlong, chinko in Japanese, titi in Filipino, whatever else people called it, cause so much commotion among so many? I grabbed onto it, closed my eyes, regretted I had not charged more, then took a deep breath, forgetting about the food that he never ordered.

Amen.

17
The New Yorker

Tokyo, 1980

The more I excelled in school, the more I cruised the hotel arcade. The more I cruised the hotel arcade, the more I must excel in school. This was the cycle that kept me in constant motion. This was the narrative that worked for my family, teachers, and classmates too, at least the part they could see. To them, I treated my school life like a full-time job, so they didn't question my motives, schedule, or whereabouts. They thought I was an overachiever. And I fully owned it.

I led my class to victory during Spirit Week when we dressed up for theme days, created class cheers, and beat the freshmen, juniors, and seniors in round robin tug-of-war. We sponsored a dance complete with multiple mirror balls and a smoke machine, a first in St. Mary's school dance history. Better yet, it broke an attendance record because I sent posters not only to Seisen and Sacred Heart, but to St. Maur in Yokohama as well, three all-girls Catholic international schools.

We took a weekend class trip to Hachijō-jima, where we cycled the entire volcanic island and scared one another with ghost stories at night. Not only was I on the Brain Bowl team but also on the Debate and Speech teams. I maintained a 3.8 GPA thanks to a few stumbles in Algebra and Geometry. I ran varsity track. I played all-night mah-jongg with my friends. All Tatay asked was that I show up with the family for Mass every Sunday morning.

I capitalized on my momentum and ran as Student Council vice-president for my coming junior year. This time all of high school voted, and I won by a landslide. In celebration, I ditched the usual afterschool outing with friends to the Game Center followed by a curry or gyudon beef bowl chow down and instead wandered off to the Imperial Hotel.

I didn't have a set pattern to my forays into the shopping arcade. Soon after my encounter with the Italian, I ventured back, mostly on weekends when I could use Student Council work or hanging out with friends as my foolproof alibi. I figured out what was clearly an established cruising spot for men seeking men. How it came to be and for how long it had been there, I had no sense of whatsoever. Though I knew it was an arena I could easily maneuver within and make work to my advantage. I learned that I could read a situation not to mention sell myself to bidders high and low.

A couple of Japanese guys in their twenties or thirties were also regulars intent on luring a guest into their hotel room. I even nodded to them in acknowledgment a few times. They returned the favor, though when we were all present, we seemed to claim territory to certain aisles and corners. I always thought I had the upper hand as my English was more coherent than theirs. And they knew it. But as far as I could tell, they were seeing enough action to keep returning to the scene of our crimes.

I was even there three afternoons in a row one spring weekend when tourists were aplenty and the shopping arcade was bustling thanks to the lure of cherry blossoms in full bloom. And it did not take long to reel in someone with my bait.

In recent months, I'd met both businessmen and tourists, a movie director and a professor, but many others hadn't been willing to give me even a hint of what they did for a living. Many said they were married, to a woman, a man (*oh?*), to God, or to their job.

Besides Stan from Auckland and Mr. Talent Scout from Milan, they hailed from Manchester, Oslo, Dusseldorf, Tel Aviv, and Melbourne. I had met more men from America than anywhere else: San Francisco, two from Los Angeles, Chicago, Atlanta, and Lubbock, a place I'd never heard of before. I tore a map out of the library atlas and marked where they were from with felt pen dots, like a head office would its satellite branches. I kept it tucked inside my knapsack.

It was all so very easy. I'd just loop around the arcade or sometimes the mezzanine with its many airline offices, until someone made eye contact and followed me into the men's room. I'd be certain of their intentions whenever they began to stroke their cocks instead of or after peeing into the urinal. I would then follow them to their rooms. Our encounters never lasted more than fifteen or twenty minutes. They usually wanted to perform oral sex on me. I loved it, and I thrived on the attention.

As soon as they came, whether I had or not, they asked me to leave. Sometimes I was more than willing to hurry things up, especially when infrequent bathing or overactive armpits made me wince if not want to puke.

Most of the time, I was able to negotiate and collect up front before I undressed or did whatever they asked. Otherwise, I left. No one had stopped me yet.

So far, I had earned 75,000 yen, which I spent eating out with friends, playing the latest video games, and going to the movies, as well as buying the occasional adult magazines from vending machines. I had hoped to see something more than female breasts and air-brushed vaginas or manko, as my Japanese-speaking classmates called them. I ended up frantically flipping through the thick manga-like bindings before I threw them in the trash.

Upon entering the arcade one Saturday afternoon in October, I was greeted by a cocktail of tea aroma, perfume, and hair salon perm solutions. It was as familiar and comforting as the damp, almost dank, tatami straw mat smell that emanated from beneath my futon at home. I figured one or two shopkeepers must recognize me by now, and if they did, they were more likely to look the other way.

They had to know part of what kept them afloat were all the foreign male guests who came here to shop, both for merchandise and for other men. And if it happened to be an Asian boy like me they were shopping for, one who was also eager to make an international connection, then we both won.

I walked into the bookstore, where I thumbed through the latest issues of *Time* and *Newsweek*, even though Tatay subscribed to both. I was thinking how all the news we got was America-centric even though the magazines were labelled International Editions. But then I caught a glimpse of a gentleman in his fifties. He stood next to me, looking at me with a forced grin, then averting his eyes to a paperback copy he held hymnal style of *The Japanese* by Edwin O. Reischauer, the gaijin's bible on understanding this enigmatic society.

I returned to my magazine and pretended to read, moving my head instead of my eyes across the page.

He spoke directly to me. "What's new in the world?"

I looked up at his round, freckled face, and wispy white hair. "More than I care to read right now."

He chuckled and just stared at me.

With a pregnant pause so early in our interaction, I felt awkward and turned back to my magazine, certain he was a dud. I have had my share of them and their silences. I gathered they could not speak English well enough to get beyond hello. Or were cagey, perhaps too fearful, or guilty to pursue anything, especially if they wore a wedding band. Or they could have been mute for all I knew. In this case, he was probably one big bore.

"I'm sorry. I just find you so attractive." *American accent, Southerner.* I had heard this pick-up line before. I wanted to blurt out pu-leez and ask him to go away. But this was part of the game. I had to play coy in order to move ahead, no matter how sophisticated he seemed, no matter how sexy he was.

"You're not bad looking yourself." It was the reply I used most which seemed to always work. I must have heard the line in a movie that I could no longer recall.

The caress of the cream sheet's threads and the plumpness of the pillows both lulled me into a catnap. Leonard snuggled his warm, fragrance-free body against my backside, my knees bent into a fetal position. I was like a stubborn jigsaw puzzle piece that had finally found its proper place.

"Ever hear of spooning?" he asked? I shrugged. We had just made each other come with our crisscrossed arms and hands, my left on his cock, his right on mine, both of us spurting in synch.

Though many of my recent trysts tended to be quick, they always concluded in bed and were followed by a static silence after that last gulp of breathlessness and damp towel wipe, when the anticipation dissipated, the tensions were released, and we could proceed along our merry separate ways. But I was not ready to break away just yet this time.

"Jobert, how're you doing?" he whispered into my ear.

"Fine, thanks. You?"

"Good, just honest to goodness good." He squeezed my chest. "This is a nice way to end my trip."

"I'm sorry you're leaving so soon."

"Me too."

"Where's home again?" I was sure I had not asked him earlier as we'd toppled onto the bed the moment I'd entered his room.

"Manhattan." *Finally, someone from New York.*

"I was just there last year with my family. I'd love to go visit again."

"You should." *Yeah, whatever.* "Like no other place in the world."

"You sound like an ad for Bloomingdale's."

He laughed. "Oh, you know about Bloomingdale's."

"It's a long story," I said. "So, tell me about yourself."

Leonard proceeded to recount his life story, and I turned around to face him. He had moved from Mississippi to Manhattan after several years of organizational consulting for oil and gas multinationals in Caracas, Jakarta, Singapore, and elsewhere. He still did so but made it a point to escape to other parts of Asia as often as he could. He had also been to Chiang Mai and Kyoto on this current trip and was headed home tomorrow. He pointed to lacquer murals and a Buddha head sculpture across the room he said he was re-packing for his flight. I was captivated by his narration, learning so much about the naked man next to me in so little time, something that had not happened much since meeting Stan.

"And what about you?" he asked.

I was more than eager to talk about all the countries I had lived in as well as my accomplishments at school. He listened intently and smiled as I carried on with my monologue.

"How old are you anyway?"

"Sixteen."

He sat up, a flash of panic in his jerky motions.

"What's wrong?" I asked. I too sat up and reached across for his shoulder.

"You said you've met men here before?"

"I won't lie, yes."

"I see. Do they find out how old you are?"

"Only if they ask. Why?"

"I don't even know the laws out here. I sure do the ones back home."

I caught his drift. The thought never fully occurred to me that I was a minor who should not be having sex with grown men. He claimed he thought I was at least eighteen or nineteen. He proceeded to tell me what age of consent was, a concept I knew nothing about. I had not considered it criminal, though I always thought when someone was apprehended in the news for sexual assault, it was due to rape or something forced and unwelcomed, hardly what was happening with me.

"Please don't make me leave," I said. "We were having such a good time."

"I've got to start packing."

"Please. I feel like I've just made a friend." I staved off tears as I patted my left hand across his back. "I mean, no one treats me well like you do."

What I really wanted to say was that although I had friends in school, I preferred to keep my ties to them along the surface. Shallow seemed safe. It had become my modus operandi if not my defense mechanism given all the moving around imposed by Tatay. Being uprooted was always a possibility, as if we were nomads when he decided it was time to search for the next oasis.

And in a strange way, making a connection with Leonard was icing on the cake of transience among all the foreign male guests I had encountered. There was a sense of safety if not comfort. None of them were repeats. There were no repercussions; little risk really with a lot of monetary reward at stake. Perhaps to Leonard's suggestion, men were willing to pay me premium for being underage. So be it. I wouldn't fully understand the notion of sexual exploitation until later. I always felt I was in control of every situation and perhaps the taking advantage of was really in reverse.

"May I ask a question?"

Leonard looked at me, expectant.

"Did you always know you were—you know…"

"You mean gay?"

I nodded. "Yes, gay."

He looked up to the ceiling. It looked like he was trying to connect dots in his head.

"It wasn't so easy to come out as gay in my time. It still isn't, though times are changing."

"I don't think so," I said. "Kids get bullied at school."

"Do you get bullied at school?"

I was going to say no but decided to change the subject. "Have you seen *Cruising* with Al Pacino?" I asked.

I had read about the movie in *Newsweek*. It was about gay murders in New York that supposedly showed a lot of what homosexuals did to hook up with one another. I would sneak into a theater later in the year the moment I saw a billboard for it by the theater not far from where Tatay worked in Shibuya.

"No, can't say I have," he replied.

"Have you ever seen any gay movies?"

Leonard propped himself up like a reclined Buddha with his open palm resting on the crown of his head, supporting a triangle that included his arm and elbow. With a closed smile, he seemed ready to enlighten me.

"Actually, I have."

"Tell me about one."

He looked up at the ceiling yet again.

"Well, there's this scene of a blond guy lying on a deserted beach sunbathing, and a man walks by." The words painted a scene which surged right back down to my groin at the speed of light. My dick stiffened. "He sees his beautiful body and goes over and starts fondling him."

"And?"

"And they kiss, then they become intimate."

"Meaning?"

"Well, um, then they make love." *Make love?*

Leonard looked under the sheet as if he knew the effect all of this was having on me.

"Tell me another story."

"Oh, okay, let me think. Yes, there are these guys trekking in the mountains who lose their way through this dense forest..."

He continued on for a few minutes more. I was rapt, conjuring up the sexy outdoor scene. But he then stopped in mid-sentence and kissed me on the lips.

"I'd rather not talk about movies when I have the real thing here."

He reached for my dick and went down on me under the covers. He made me come once more before we agreed to take a nap. He rewrapped his arms around me. Halfway between awake and asleep, I transposed myself onto a shore, where the blues of sky and ocean melded on the horizon, where the blond guy waved at me to come over. As I closed in, he stood up sporting light blue Speedos. He reached for my hand and pulled me in for a long wet kiss. And we made love, whatever it entailed.

Leonard was fast asleep when I woke up to darkness outside at 18:30 according to my Seiko. He snored lightly on the back of my ear. Although I thought about asking him for money before I headed home, I ultimately decided to accept all he had shared with me that afternoon as payment enough.

18
Chemistry

Tokyo, 1980

Helmut pressed his heel against my chair. This was my signal to get the sheet, folded in fours, from behind without looking back as I would with a baton as the second leg in a relay race. I scanned the indents down the page: C, C, A, B, D, A. I was six for six.

"Time's up. Pens down. Now," said Miss Faggins, her beaded dreadlocks swishing from side to side like little Medusa snakes. "All answers on my desk in thirty seconds or else." *Or else?*

Her childish tone fueled suspicion that she was only our new chemistry teacher because St. Mary's was desperate to fill the post left vacant in the spring and would have hired whoever came along. The first term of our junior year was well underway, and parents had begun to complain that there was no one to teach chemistry. And then she showed up with an acidic pH on her face.

I offered to take Helmut's, John's, Seung Poon's and Han Jun's sheets up to her. The classroom emptied out into recess, as much to get away from Miss Faggins and her pop quizzes as to devour the day's lunch special, spaghetti and meatballs. I returned to clear my desk and dispose of our circle's cheat sheet when I realized Helmut's quiz was stuck to it.

Oh, fuck!

I ran back up. "Miss Faggins, sorry, here's one more."

She glanced at Helmut's quiz, put it in the pile, and scowled at me before grabbing her shoulder bag and walking out the door. I swear I heard her hair rattle.

We knew cheating could lead to suspension if not expulsion, just as possessing drugs meant deportation out of Japan as it happened with a senior classman last spring. We were all honor roll students who didn't have to resort to such risky behavior. Granted, we didn't prepare for her class the way we did biology, and Miss Faggins's quizzes counted for only a third of our grade. Maybe it was our collective dislike for her literally by-the-textbook teaching method, apathetic posture, or laughable last name. Whatever it was, it had nothing to do with her being Black, though I overheard some of the troublemakers in class make racist jokes behind her back.

I did not want to alarm my friends about the near disaster with Helmut's quiz. Though our one serious attempt at cheating needed to end there. I trusted and cared for my friends, though I was sure they wouldn't be as chummy if they found out I made money taking my clothes off and performing sexual favors for foreign men. I would have had myself deported on the spot rather than face the humiliation. I was certain no one knew. Or that anyone suspected. These were separate worlds I alone traversed with care, some cunning, and, most of all, confidence.

Still the devil in me dared to risk even more.

Every Thursday was lab day. Miss Faggins filed her nails as we carried out experiments from our workbooks. Wearing our goggles, we measured and observed, recorded and interpreted the reactions of various elements, most of it oxidization. We secretly strived for explosions that would cause everyone else in the lab to applaud.

We were clustered in fours. By the luck of first day seating, Helmut, John, and I were in the same cluster, along with Curt, a new arrival from Sydney, Australia. He and I sat next to one another and took turns washing out our equipment at the end of each lab session.

Once I inserted the bristly brush, a bonsai version of what was used to clean toilet bowls, into a test tube with such force, it splashed suds all over Curt's gold curls and chalky cheeks.

"Oops. Sorry."

"It's okay," he laughed before splattering me with water from a beaker. He then jutted his face out with eyes closed and lips pursed for me to wipe him up, first with my hands, and then with a paper towel. I went with and against the grain of his day-old facial hair. I had to lean against the sink to conceal my instant hard-on. And I wanted to believe he was doing the same.

Just as I had developed an intuition for the men walking about aimlessly in the hotel arcade, I did so with Curt. For weeks I was an electron in constant orbit around him, the nucleus of my attention, observing him and logging notes in my mental notebook to see if I could have arrived at any conclusions to my hypothesis on whether he was into other boys as well.

He took an Australian correspondence course in Economics and, therefore, used his last school period to study in the library while the rest of us were in history class. He often won breaststroke and butterfly events at swimming meets. The word "tasty" came to mind every time I saw him in his skimpy, St. Mary's Titan-blue Speedos. I once walked into the locker room to interview him on the pretense that it was for *The Diplomat*, our school paper. He was happy to answer my questions, unaware of my glances at his towel knotted below his folded arms, defined chest, and pinpoint belly button. I fantasized grabbing the towel off him.

In one of our lab sessions, I was in a babbling mood. "You look good today," I said. I was referring to his yellow sweater vest. Along with his navy tie and blazer made him even more handsome, more preppy, a word that had recently come into my consciousness after having read about *The Official Preppy Handbook* in *Time* and *Newsweek*.

"Thanks," he said. For a moment, I was almost certain his woolen knee brushed mine.

"You look like a living doll," I added.

To this, he looked away then back at me. His face turned an intense shade of magenta, undoubtedly a chemical reaction. At a loss for words, perhaps, he dropped his head toward his workbook. I felt a jerk and shrinking sensation inside of me. *Eew. What did I just say?* Thank god the others had not heard our exchange. We were silent for the rest of the day's lab experiment. In my head, I argued both sides for why he may or may not be gay. I may have just blown my cover with my asinine comment, though. *Who calls another guy a living doll?* This was good, I rationalized, but there was more downside than upside to what had just transpired. He could have freaked out and let everyone know what I just said and therefore intimate that I was a fag? But wouldn't that have been just as much a risk for him as well? I wasn't so sure anymore. I flagellated myself in my mind and decided to avoid contact with Curt altogether when outside the lab.

He and I continued to carry out our class experiments week after week with skill, a bit more distance and good marks on our reports, the second third of our grade. Curt remained gregarious. though he did not seem to stray off script. As for me, I tried to get inside his head, believing he knew what I thought I knew, what we both knew, and what was perhaps going on between us.

For the next few weeks, whenever I hooked up with someone at the hotel, I could not help but replace the face and body I was attending to with that of Curt's. A forty or fifty something turned sixteen in my mind's eye, and I could come right then and there. One Saturday afternoon, when I was supposed to be with my friends sneaking into adults only pachinko parlors in Shibuya, I walked up and down the arcade for three hours and was unable to make any contact, with the exception of two Asian men, likely Taiwanese or Singaporean, each an hour apart. They were non-verbally aggressive in getting me to follow them to their rooms, but I ignored them. I panicked for a moment and looped around the arcade even faster but was soon resigned to going home with a strike to my perfect streak so to speak.

Part of me wished I had done something else with my afternoon. My buddies had probably seen a movie I would then miss out on talking about. They would have had breaded pork tonkatsu or yakisoba; maybe even slurped down a big bowl of ramen, the thought of which made me hungry. Thoughts of Curt were squarely parked inside of me as I tried to find a way for him to be comfortable enough around me to say or be anything he wanted. I headed home, thinking it might have been worth giving up all the men and energy I expended at the Imperial Hotel for a steady boyfriend like Curt.

Like I said, part of me dared to risk even more.

The semester was soon ending, and the last of our lab sessions was at hand. I made one last ditch attempt to get Curt's attention by swallowing a crystal blue granule of sodium nitrate. I did it as a bet to my cluster mates, thinking that a salt used as a fertilizer and in curing meat could not be that harmful.

"Oh my," said Curt as he put his hand to his mouth the moment I popped the compound into my mouth.

Helmut and John were flabbergasted as well.

"Mm...quite good," I said as I then stuck my tongue out at them for inspection.

Seconds later, an itch flared up into a flame and soon a wildfire spread through my throat.

"Water," I said, running out the door while the rest of the class looked on to see what the commotion was about. Miss Faggins remained focused on her cuticles.

I stopped at the water fountain by the boy's room and took loud gulps down my throat until I felt a bloat in my stomach. With each swallow, the piercing sensation intensified then disappeared before starting up again. It felt like a stubborn shard of glass that would not wash down. I headed for the toilet where I hacked until spit mixed in with cereal and yogurt regurgitated from within.

Fuck me. What a loser.

A few shades redder, I wiped my involuntary tears and gargled at the sink. I wanted to return to the lab as if nothing had happened.

"Are you okay?" Curt asked, rather concerned, or so I read into his intonation.

"Yeah," I said almost in a whisper.

"That was funny, but not too smart," he said.

I wanted to grab him by the shoulders and shake him, to say something, anything, even if it was moronic and revealing like, "I did it because I want you to open up to me, okay? Pay attention to me, desire me as I do you." But then the consequence of having to leave St. Mary's out of shame, railroading my tenure as vice-president, draining all my accomplishments down the sink, being a school pariah, and having to face my parents, all such thoughts loomed heavy.

"I learned my lesson," I said.

His eyes were celadon green, cool and ceramic-like. I peered into them long enough for me, not him, to feel discomfort and look away. Little was said thereafter for the rest of class and for the remainder of the semester. For another year and a half, until we graduated, we would be cordial. And nothing more. Until then, I carried my longing for Curt with me wherever I went like an amulet that would protect me from all harm.

I received a note in the mail from Leonard written on thick ivory stationery with his calligraphic initials in an envelope without a return address. He wished me Happy Holidays and said he looked forward to seeing me when he was to return in March. Mommy asked whom the letter was from. I told her it was a St. Mary's alum who was to speak to members of the National Honor Society about college options in New York come March when he would visit St. Mary's and that details were forthcoming from Mr. Hauet. We left it at that.

Finals, of which constituted the last third of our chemistry grade, were the remaining hurdle that separated us from Christmas break. We were in the midst of study days. I had lost all motivation to memorize chemical symbols and equations. I turned to flashcards and pneumonic devices, which meant I would forget everything by the following semester.

My grades still remained in the top ten percentile, mostly As and A-s. I rationalized that being on the new International Baccalaureate track offered a degree of added difficulty, so to me, my B+ was more like an A-. Though lurking in the background was the ingrained pressure that anything B+ or below was really an Asian F.

But what distracted me from all of this was that I was horny, and I knew how to satiate it. To get my fix. Back at the Imperial Hotel.

An ersatz scene of a snowman with a samurai's sword and a red sleigh full of electronics greeted me as I enter the hotel's arcade. This was not unlike the way most of Tokyo dressed up for the holidays.

Children posed with a gaijin Santa at Mitsukoshi, Matsuya, Takashimaya, Seibu, and Tokyu, to name some of the top department stores my family frequented. Their lower level food sections offered Christmas strawberry shortcakes, no larger than a toy drum, which with a large barrel of Kentucky Fried Chicken, and a quick exchange of gifts, was the extent many Japanese families observed *Ku-ri-su-ma-su*.

I was in the hotel arcade in search of sex as I had been for over a year, maybe two. I must have been in here a hundred times, or so it felt. I turned the corners without looking at window displays or passersby, just the carpet floor, its fibers and specks. *No, I don't need the money. There's no cause for celebration. I have a Chemistry final in two days. Curt will never be my boyfriend. My parents think I'm a boy wonder at school. I'll never have a boyfriend. I want to be Student Council President next. I'll never be happy. I am parading as a fraud in front of the whole world.*

I peed in the men's room. Someone was already standing at the far end urinal, as if he had been expecting me. I did not even care how old he was or where he was from or what his life was like. He was going to be just another trick. As long as he sucked my cock and paid me for doing so, that was all I needed to keep me going.

I almost forget about the Christmas concert and all-school Mass in the gymnasium on the last day before classes were finally let out at lunchtime and for the holidays. A bunch of us were going to head to the game center, see a movie, and play mah-jongg.

Our Chemistry finals were available in the lab, in white envelopes with our names. A D+ bled across the top of mine. I folded it back up and tossed it in my knapsack. As I added this to an A- for lab reports and a B- for quizzes then divided by three. That gave me a final course grade of C.

My first C. My very first C.

I told my friends I would be right behind them as I sat alone in our classroom. I took a deep breath before mulling over my final, hoping Miss Faggins had made a terrible mistake.

I then tried to find consolation in the fact that C stood for Curt, but that notion evaporated quickly. How would I explain it to my parents? And will it jeopardize my chances of getting into a good college? I wondered whether I could have done better had I spent less time at the Imperial Hotel and more on my studies. Whatever the conclusion, it was too late to matter. It was a scarlet letter on my transcript. Yet it would not stop me from returning to the Imperial Hotel.

I took the envelope out of my knapsack, tore it up, and tossed it in a trash bin. I then walked in the opposite direction from my friends toward a different train station, still not ready to head home.

19

Yokohama Yoshiko

Tokyo/Yokohama, 1981

Bodies bounced and bumped under mirror balls that spewed beads of light in all directions to the cranked up choral catch phrase: *toot-toot-hey-beep-beep*. Glass sliding doors which led into the courtyard and ran the entire length of the cafeteria by day were locked, fogged up and even sweating with condensation. Some drew initials and arrow-pierced hearts with their fingers, others wrote insults and vulgar language like "fag" and "pussy." *Oh how original.* Mr. Montgomery, our homeroom teacher-cum-history teacher-cum-basketball coach-cum-chaperone signaled "stop" then wiped off the atmospheric graffiti with his palms. There was whistling, howling, singing, and line dancing. It was 10:35, and the crowd swelled before the last few numbers spun and another school dance would be history by 11:00 p.m.

I knew Donna Summer's "Bad Girls" really referred to prostitutes, hookers, whores, harlots, tramps, sluts, and whatever else the library thesaurus labelled them. Some of my classmates bragged that they have had one or more, sex creatures that swarmed the disco districts of Harajuku, Shinjuku, and Roppongi targeting rich kids and gaijins. I was told they gave good head, liked to do it doggy-style, and did not cost much money. Then it dawned on me. I was a Bad Boy myself.

"Bad Girls" faded out as Blondie's "Call Me" cranked up. I tapped my foot, still standing by the door as I had all night with my casual slouch, overseeing the pay-and-stamp table and making nicey-nicey with my constituents given I was Student Council vice-president recently turned president-elect for my senior year.

But I was also a Bad Boy who had the Imperial Hotel arcade as my strip, my street. But with "Call Me," my thoughts floated to one afternoon when I went into a theater instead to salivate over Richard Gere in *An American Gigolo*. I had seen his face in the *Newsweek* "Newsmakers" page and had heard the movie's theme song on Casey Kasem's *American Top 40* on Armed Forces Radio.

I had not fully appreciated what it meant to be a gigolo, a word I had not even bothered to look up its definition in the school library, but as the credits rolled, and I emerged into the bright of day, I said to myself *I want to be Richard Gere*. In a way, I already was, but unlike his character, it was men I slept with for hard, cold cash.

"Hi, care to dance?"

I turned to face a girl, slightly shorter, with wiry hair and slits for eyes. Her smile was a lipless line of sheer determination.

"Ah, sure," I replied.

We walked to the center of the dance floor dodging elbows and sidestepping toes then shook our bodies amongst the throngs. I gyrated as I saw others do, really with themselves and not necessarily with their partners. Two thoughts wrestled in me. One, I had never been asked to dance by a girl before. *Who is she anyway?* Two, I had never been to the Imperial Hotel late at night when the stores were already closed. I wondered whether men cruised this late. Maybe I would head there after the dance was done, so I phoned my parents to say I was off with the gang to John's place for a mah-jongg sleepover.

As "Call Me" gave way to The Knack's "My Sharona," she gave me an infectious smile. She looked at me, then away, then back, and our eyes locked. I could not help but smile back. We then made underwater scuba moves. We got down and grooved. We let go a little, our pace as frenetic as the beat.

"What's your name?" I shouted.

"Yo-shi-ko!"

"Jo-bert!" I offered a handshake that she firmly grabbed.

"I know. I saw you in Brain Bowl. I'm on the Saint Maur team," she yelled into my ear.

"Really? Nice to meet you."

"You too."

"You were great in *Arsenic and Old Lace*. Loved Dr. Einstein."

"Oh you saw?" I was still receiving accolades for my comedic role in the school play last December. Late rehearsals proved the perfect cover up for more Imperial Hotel escapades.

Yoshiko and I returned to our solo moves, only this time we made more eye contact. My eardrums were ready to pop. The DJ's transition from "My Sharona" to the latter, more danceable half of Donna Summer's "Last Dance" was seamless, and we kept on dancing.

Then the song stopped and the spotlights dimmed, their cellophane filters fading from orange and red to blue and purple as the mirror ball beads still did their dance. The piercing keyboard chords of Little River Band's ballad, "Cool Change," reverberated throughout the entire room.

The last dance was always a slow dance.

Yoshiko looked at me, almost longingly. I took her hands and gently hoisted them on my shoulders before wrapping mine around the small of her wet back. She smelled of sweet soap. Soon her head was heavy against my chest, as if in search of my heartbeat.

As the song faded and the cafeteria's harsh lights came on, we reluctantly peeled away from one another.

"Thanks," she said. "By the way, we have a dance Saturday after next at our school. Would you like to come?"

"Sure. I've never been to your school anyway."

"I'll call you this week with details," she said.

I scribbled down my phone number on the way out and waved goodnight as she rejoined her chums, all zipping up their jackets and cackling, teasing her as she turned to cast one last glance my way. My friends gave me knowing looks with their arched eyebrows, nothing more.

I wrapped up my Student Council duties overseeing the crew that stored the last of the music and light equipment as well as counting the wad of five hundred and thousand yen bills, not bad for a school dance on a cold early spring night. Upon handing the money box over to Mr. Montgomery, I then joined my friends for a bowl of soba noodles before parting ways at the train station. It was almost midnight. They were off to John's for the second half of the night. As I reached the platform, I changed my mind and headed home instead to sleep in my own room.

I trekked out to Yokohama, with detailed directions from Yoshiko in hand. It was a lot farther away from the train station than I had allowed for. I hastened my pace, partly because I was late, and partly because I was cold, but most of all I was anxious. I followed the music to the St. Maur school cafeteria and upon my arrival, Yoshiko dashed to greet me, as if she had been on constant lookout since the dance started an hour and a half ago.

"You made it," she said. She was in a baby blue wool blouse that set off her glazed complexion. I detected a hint of blush. *Doesn't St. Maur have a no makeup policy like the others?* A fine gold chain with a small crucifix dangled halfway between her pointy-bra breasts.

"Glad to be here. Thanks for inviting me."

It had been a whole two weeks since we met, and I had not returned to the Imperial Hotel, either. I had been busy with Advanced Biology and forward planning my agenda as Student Council president. Yoshiko and I had chitchatted on the phone for an hour once while my parents were away. In a way, it was a relief, a nice change of pace not having to invest—or waste—up to three hours at a time to find a john at the hotel arcade.

Yoshiko took me by the hand and paraded me over to meet her friends. As I greeted each of them, they flashed knowing grins. We made small talk about other boys at St. Mary's, and I saw they had more than just a passing interest. And throughout, thoughts randomly popped in me like kernels of corn. *I like her. She likes me. I like men. I like dick. I've never fucked a vagina. We're playing boyfriend-girlfriend.*

And just like that, I returned her grip, to the point our palms perspired. Yes, I did find her pretty and smart and assertive, which I liked. She obviously liked me. Sparks were not flying the way they did in the arcade, but that was okay. It was nice to know girls found me attractive. It served as a sort of protective armor for my masculinity.

We danced for two hours straight to many of the same songs that played back at St. Mary's, though there were no slow dances. She and I took only one break so we could each go to the bathroom as well as have some overly sweet punch and flirt some more, under the watchful eyes of habit-headed nun chaperones.

Yoshiko insisted on walking me back to the train station. We held hands all the way there. I wanted to do the gentlemanly thing and escort her back home since she said she lived within walking distance, but she refused. Instead, she wanted to ensure I got on the right train and back home safely.

It was my turn. I kissed her on the cheek and lightly on the lips. Her eyes remained closed as I pulled away. That was enough for one night. And really for the rest of the semester as I found a multitude of excuses not to see her again until her graduation. After all, she didn't do it for me. As much as I enjoyed being with her, and all the other girls preceding her, I doubt I ever had a genuine hard on for any of them.

"Jobert's got a girlfriend. Jobert's got a girlfriend," Rossana sang out at the dinner table the Monday after.

"I do not," I insisted, though unconvincingly, even to myself. My sister had heard rumors at her school, International School of the Sacred Heart, which reminded me how word travels fast across all the Catholic international schools, especially when it came to dating gossip.

Mommy looked at me for more details. Tatay grinned, sporting lots of teeth, and gave me a fatherly punch to my arm, a rare, sporadic event like the return of Halley's comet, before he finished the rest of his ice cream. All seemed good in his universe, not to mention mine. I had a dark secret to hide, and everything I did to conceal it seemed to be going according to plan.

20

Sleep Over/Overslept

Tokyo, 1981

I picked up my pace on the escalator and through the turnstile. It swallowed my ticket stub and spewed it out the other end for the return trip home. My thoughts moved even faster. I was unable to focus, unable to grab on to any one fragment of the jostling between anticipation and anxiety within me.

I popped a mint to combat my fiery breath after having inhaled yakisoba and ginger garnish at the standup noodle kiosk in the Futako Tamagawa train station, not far from school. It had been another victorious all-Saturday track and field meet. But I was running late. Seiko check: 18:10. I exited the subway, entered the arcade, and scaled the stairway two steps at a time toward the hotel lobby without as much a glance at any of the shops or shoppers. I groped the phone receiver, coiling its black corkscrew cord tight around my index finger. It turned red followed by a lifeless white as I released it.

"Guest please. Leonard C_____." The operator must have thought me angry given my heaving and spittle-ridden delivery. A minute's eternity ticked by.

"Hello, Leonard? Jobert here. I'm downstairs."

"Jobert. Hurry on up. Room 1406."

I fidgeted with my hair and madras shirt all the way to his room. What was supposed to occur in the glory of March turned into an ambivalent April that had become a blistering May. For a while, I thought the postponements were his way of saying I don't care to see you ever again. But why would he have gone through the trouble of sending notes with multiple promises to let me know when he'd actually return to Tokyo, which only raised Mommy's suspicion every time another letter arrived: a New York postmark, my name in calligraphic strokes on ivory parchment, postage stamps with an L and a skewed O sitting atop a V and E, and no return address?

Leonard welcomed me at the door with an embrace that felt more fatherly than from someone I had had sex with and expected to have with again momentarily.

"It's good to see you," he said. He gestured for me to sit on the couch adjacent to him. "What's it been? Six months?"

"More like a year," I replied.

He looked out the window onto the slight haze at the Imperial Palace and its moat, as if he should have known better. Or perhaps he was wondering where time flies.

"You mentioned you're off to Laos, right?" I asked.

"Yes, and Angkor Wat in Cambodia as well," he said. "Over a week before I head to Jakarta for meetings."

"How long are you here for?"

"Overnight. I fly out to Bangkok tomorrow."

"Oh, just a stopover I see." I disguised my disappointment as best I could.

"I wanted to see how you were doing."

"Oh...well, I'm here." I mockingly pointed at myself from head to toe as if I was a brand new refrigerator to be won by a lucky member of the studio audience.

"You look good. Exercising a lot?"

"Yeah, track season."

"And how are your studies going?"

"Okay, thanks." I needed not bother him with my grade in Chemistry. Nor Analytical Geometry. I was headed toward another C on my transcript.

"Jobert, do you still make it to Mass on Sundays?"

I chuckled. One, he remembered me mentioning this, and two, why this line of questioning?

"Do you still come here often?"

"You mean the hotel? Not much lately. Maybe once in a while." That was a lie as coming to the hotel was pretty much a weekly occurrence. I also need not fill him in on Yoshiko, who I was believed to be dating as far as others were concerned, thus quelling any suspicions over my sexuality.

"Are you being careful?" *Careful about what?* "Do you carry condoms with..."

"Look. I appreciate your concern and all, but I'm doing just fine as you can see. I'm careful." *I don't get fucked, period.*

I was beginning to read reports in *Newsweek* of homosexual Americans contracting a virus and dying. Something to do with anal sex.

"I wasn't prying," said Leonard. "It's just that these days...it's just that I consider you a friend, that's all. I want you to be protected."

"And I you, but I have a father and mother to contend with as is," I snapped back. It was my turn to look out the window, more at the twilight sky than the cityscape, until bubbles, my eye doctor called them floaters, danced back and forth. I squinted and shut my eyes.

"Jobert, it's good to see you. Truly." He seemed apologetic as he dropped his chin to his chest.

"It's good to see you too, Leonard." An uncomfortable silence settled between us, not unlike the very first time we met.

"Can we just nap a while?" I asked. "You must be jet-lagged."

I still held out hope sex would ensue and that it would be just as satisfying the second time around.

"I wouldn't mind a few winks," he said, as he, yeah, winked.

He walked over to the bed, pulled down the covers, dimmed the lamp, located classical music on the console, and drew the curtains shut. The room's metamorphosis was complete. I undressed except for my underwear and slipped into the perfect sheets. Leonard followed in his boxer shorts.

We wrapped our arms around each other, our warm bodies like two slices of toast slapped together to be spread with peanut butter and jam. He was not wearing any cologne and smelled of neutrality. He swirled his finger up my back and over to my scalp. He located pressure points on my skull that elicited a purr out of me. It was as if the past eleven months had been nothing more than a brief intermission.

"Where were we?" he asked.

"I'm not sure."

"Neither am I."

He turned me around so that he could spoon me. He tightened his grip around my waist and soon, in a sleepy release, emitted his trademark whispering snores.

I also heard my subdued breaths along with the whirl of central air conditioning. I had not thought much of anything as I stared up at the ceiling. My attention wandered over to the music, wondering where I had heard it before. Violin chords floated into what appeared in my mind as a lake shellacked by morning mist. There was a lone rower raising his arm, his finger in anticipation of a breeze. He curved his palm over his brows to see how much farther he must go, or whether to turn and return to dock. It was not long before I was fast asleep.

Leonard was already shaved and showered when I heard the determined knock at the door. "Room service."

I cowered under the sheets, then I followed the rattle of morning silver and coffee cups to the other end of the room, the exchange of a tip and a thank you, and the "all clear" of the closing door.

"Good morning. How'd you sleep?" he asked.

Seiko check: 5:17. *a.m.! Shit. I stayed out all night.* "I've got to go."

I started crafting my alibi as I dressed, gargled, pomaded my hair with water, and checked my profiles for any telling signs. I continued to search for an excuse as I hastily hugged and thanked Leonard who offered to stay in touch. I revised and refined my reason for staying out all night—I lost track of time at a victory party and missed the last train—and ran through my mental Rolodex of friends I could enlist as corroborators.

The train emerged out of the subway tunnel and into the early Sunday haze for the latter half of my trip home. The sun was a sour ball floating above house and apartment rooftops with TV antennae that had the silhouettes of praying mantises. With a few exceptions, home windows were like dark screens, each a channel that was about to start transmission and broadcast the day's programming

I didn't have time to ponder my reunion with Leonard until I was walking home from the train station. We did not have sex, but we slept well in each other's arms. I was disappointed, but I was also elated about where we stood as friends. As confidants. Friends who would call upon the other in times of need, or just to find out how life was going; friends who accepted each other for all of who we were without reservation.

As I tiptoed into the vestibule at just after 7:00, I heard a shuffle from above, and heavy footsteps descended the stairwell.

Mommy was barefoot and in a rumpled nightgown. She plopped herself on the last stair from where I stood, unable to utter a word. Though the story was clearly etched in her tear-drenched locks and asthmatic sobs.

"I was up all night. Worried sick. You should have called."

I was barely able to let out an "I'm sorry." She didn't ask me any questions, even though I had a lame excuse lined up about losing track of time playing mah-jongg with my classmates, the phone not working, and the trains having stopped running a bit early.

In her bloodshot eyes, I knew our relationship as mother and son had forever transformed. She rubbed them before heading back to her room. And I to mine.

Even if she suspected the truth, chances were she would first deny it, then keep it to herself and just pray for it to go away.

21

Admission

Tokyo, 1982

March 4, 1982
Tokyo, Japan

Dear Jobert:

On your eighteenth birthday today, your mother and I give you all our love and fondest wishes for the future. We give you the love we've had for you from the time we knew our prayers for a second child, a boy, had been answered at long last, some seven years after Lanelle came. Like hers, your birth gave us great joy. You should have seen me crazily handing out cigars in my office. Our love for you now is compounded by the love you've given us in return. Yes, as they say, love is boundless, and it seems to grow as you give and receive it.

Eighteen years have gone by quickly. And yet each has been so full for all of us. Full of life, growing, learning, and living—in a number of countries.

Yesterday I remembered it was 1946 when I turned eighteen. That was two years in the wake of World War II and much less it seemed after Papa and Mama died—he at 51 and she at 44. As of now, you've been with me and your mother longer than I had been with Papa and Mama, and even much longer than your mother had been with her own parents, because she was orphaned even earlier than I. In 1946, all seven of us orphans faced a future of uncertainty and insecurity, but thank God, without fear or bitterness, and with our love and humor intact. Grandma and our uncles and aunts gave us their loving support. With everyone trying hard, we somehow managed. Your Tito Teddy held us together with a vision of the best education we could, and did, get at the

153

University of the Philippines. He and your Tita Neny worked to help us onward from the province to Manila and UP. We have always believed Papa and Mama in heaven were looking after and interceding for us. Without them, we'd never be what and where we are, then and now.

As your parents, we have watched and helped in the best way we know, your development since childhood. We can only say in a few words how truly blessed all of us have been in living and growing up together. Yes, even parents do and should grow up if only to keep up with their loved ones. We have seen your God-given gifts blossom as you applied yourself with admirable effort and enthusiasm and success. Your knowledge and understanding of the world around you, enhanced by your travel and life abroad and by good schools and modern communication, surpass what we your parents could ever obtain in our time. We are grateful for all these bounties our children have enjoyed. For these and much more, we must always thank the Lord. Our best and utmost strivings cannot possibly be as fruitful without his blessings. This is one of the first things your mother and I would like all of you children to know and remember at all times. We also should be thankful for the love and generosity of your own uncles and aunties, and your growing friendships.

So Job, we go on our wonderful journey in life together, as well as individually, with our hopes and our prayers that we may be worthy of what we seek, not only for ourselves but also for the good of others. Certainly, among the lessons we each should have learned is that true happiness and fulfillment can only come through helping and caring for others, especially those who have much less in life than we. Even in your youth, you have already shown this by your example. I would like you to pursue your interest and commitment, so early developed, in serving your country and region in the future. What you are doing now at school and with your many friends in the international schools of Japan, and your study of Japanese, will prepare you for such a task and for service to humanity as a whole.

Your mother, and I'm sure Lanelle, Rossana, and Jonas, join me in greeting you: "Happy Birthday, Sweet Boy!" May you and all of us be pleasing to the Lord in spite of ourselves and because we try, as much as we humanly can, to follow him.

Love,
Tatay

Whenever Mr. Hauet added an entry to the "Congratulations!" column on the bulletin board outside his office, a hush overcame the hallway. For those few moments while his blue magic marker squeaked with every cursive stroke across the cheerful, yellow poster paper, we held the air in our chests, our feet bolted to the floor. As soon as he was gone, we flocked in from all directions, jostling, like pigeons to crumbs, eager to find out which lucky bastard got in where.

"M.I.T.! Bill K____! Again! No way!"

Whoever cried out was right. It was a two-way race between Francis L_____ and Bill K____, valedictorian and salutatorian to be, respectively. Stanford. Yale. Princeton. Cal Tech. And now M.I.T. Some got into their safety schools while most of us had yet to hear from anyone at all. It was late April, and most of the cherry blossoms lacing St. Mary's and all of Tokyo had fallen to the ground as dead confetti. Graduation was just five weeks away.

I joined the fray because I wanted to live vicariously through every triumph of my classmates. By now, my fate was pretty much sealed. Even though I had put in an application to the University of Michigan, a last-minute effort, I was trying to psych myself up to enter the University of the Philippines.

Tatay was adamant I return home for college. Throughout high school, he had taken steps to pave the way for my eventual homecoming. Our family had spent every summer back in Manila to reconnect with friends and relatives. And each trip back always included a visit to the U.P. campus. In October I took a special trip back to Manila just to sit through the National College Entrance Exams required for admission into U.P. I did not even think to sabotage my score.

Tatay was U.P. and U.P. was Tatay. He and every one of his siblings graduated from there. He met Mommy there. He was tenured there. In a decade, he would become its president.

He had little tolerance for the Michigan application, despite having received his master's and doctorate degrees from there. His son was following in his footsteps and, I feared, in his shadow as well.

On May 2, 1982 at 6:05 p.m., four weeks before graduation, in the vestibule of our house, I tore open the envelope postmarked from Ann Arbor and held the letter, shaking, mouthing each word as if I was learning to read for the very first time.

Dear Jobert:

On behalf of the Board of Regents and admissions committee I would like to welcome you...

"Mr. Hauet," I yelled into the phone. "Take out your magic marker!"

"Wow, Congratulations, Jobert."

I was conscious of the extra stretch in my smile and bounce in my sole as I walked down the St. Mary's hallways. My teachers and classmates seemed genuinely pleased for me, but then they knew I was destined to be at U.P. even though Mr. Hauet never listed my admission there for all to see.

I carried my Michigan admissions letter everywhere. I stole glances at it and quietly caressed the university's emblem, which had an oil lamp not unlike that of Aladdin's, embossed on the parchment. I fantasized what life was like on the Ann Arbor campus, figuring out ways to approach my father on actually attending college there. When he first heard the news, he smiled then changed the subject, asking what I might want to study, saying that he knew most of the professors in the College of Arts and Sciences at U.P.

Mr. Hauet wide-crossed his legs while seated at his chair facing away from his desk as I laid out my dilemma. Up until the day before I heard from Michigan, he seemed supportive. But then he was somewhat muted, maybe wanting to wash the good news off his hands. I did not ask whether he and Tatay had had a conversation.

"There are lots of factors to consider," he said, I could hear the backpedaling scratches in his voice. It was not the voice of the guidance counselor I had come to trust.

"Lots of factors? True, but you know how I feel about U.P. For God's sake, we lived outside the Philippines for almost half my life." My eyes welled up. "I'm not the son he wants me to be. Fuck. He doesn't know me."

Mr. Hauet was not taken aback by my use of the swear word. He patted my shoulder with his perspiring palm. "Now, now. Don't be so hard on yourself again. Just, well, talk to your father. Tell him how you feel. Do you ever tell him how you feel?"

"Mr. Hauet, please!" I rolled my eyes. "Fathers and sons aren't supposed to talk their feelings out. That's what makes the world a wonderful place."

I thought of how I had avoided several father-son moments throughout the years. There was an unspoken unease about talking to him about anything beyond my achievements at school. But then Tatay was always on the go, achieving on his own as well, all his life – authoring books, winning distinctions, guest lecturing at universities throughout the world, taking on plum expat assignments, and making his children global citizens. Our collective achievements spoke for themselves. What else was there really to say?

Mr. Hauet knowingly gritted his teeth at my sarcasm. "Well then, just do what you can."

"Thanks, as always," I said, then sighed. "God, if anyone knew what a cry baby I am. How many times has it been now?"

He guffawed. "Seven hundred and eight."

"Ha, ha. Very funny."

"Remember the time you lost the debate all-star standing by one point? You felt you were robbed?'

"You mean the time I demanded a recount, and found the calculation error?"

"And you got your all-star."

"How humiliating. I had to whine to win."

"But you did. And what about when you wanted to be Student Council Vice-President then President and made it happen?" I check off in my head all my other transcript enhancers. "And now you are a rare All-Sar across Brain Bowl, Debate and Speech. And track!"

"Thank you," I mustered.

"That's the essence of the Jobert Abueva I've known all these years," he added.

I cracked a grin, half-embarrassed. I then mentioned the poster Mr. Hauet gave me during my sophomore year. It still hung in my bedroom. I woke up every day to the man running a long, hilly route. It was the one I first saw in the room adjacent to his office when he asked me to sit in the group interview with *The Japan Times*: the race is not always to the swift, but to those who keep on running.

"Tatay, I think that Michigan would be a good school to attend." The words dripped out of my mouth like syrup as I refused to lock eyes with his.

"What's wrong with U.P.?"

"Nothing's wrong with U.P. It's just that I would like to experience an American education."

"That's exactly why I want you to attend U.P. You're Filipino."

"But I really feel out of place there." He sat silent, his arms crossed. I imagined us in a fierce game of battleship. D6. Kaboom. I had just sunk one of Tatay's smaller ships. It was now his turn.

"Do you have any idea what you might want to do in life?" he asked. It was more like he had pulled the pin off a grenade, ready to lob it in my direction. "Any desire to help our country?"

He was playing the nationalism chip. Sure, I was born in Manila. My roots were Filipino. Yes, I enjoyed overwrought Filipino films and could not care less about the cholesterol in the fat suckling lechon sumptuously roasting on a spitfire or its strained blood and innards pureed in dinuguan. I had the most Filipino sweet tooth for maja blanca, halo-halo and buttery sans rival cake. But I had also tasted life abroad and got a whiff of America's allure. Independence. Opportunity. Affluence. Sexual freedom. And as much as the Philippines needed a reverse brain drain and had to progress despite a Marcos dictatorship, I did not think I belonged there. *You don't know it yet. I am gay. And I can't be myself and still be an Abueva.*

"Of course I want to help the Philippines," I said. "This is only college we're talking about."

"Where your network will be established?"

"The world is my network. I've moved everywhere you've made me go. For once I want to go somewhere I want to go." I was on the verge of losing my temper if not having a breakdown, the kind with high-pitched wails and flailing arms ready to throw anything within reach across the room. E7. A direct hit.

"Job, you can't call every shot."

"I want to go to Michigan, okay?" I was beyond flustered.

Tatay turned silent again. I could sense his mind was working on overdrive trying to maintain calm, careful not to make this conversation disintegrate into raw emotions as we had done a few times in the past. It was all too easy. We both knew it. We were of the same blood, yet still like oil and water.

"Why did I even bother applying?" I yelled. "You should have stopped me. You could have. Why didn't you, like you always have before?"

His body shriveled somewhat and looked helpless. Almost scared at my shrillness. I took the admissions letter from Michigan up to our faces and ripped it in half. "There. Happy?" I had lost control. And all my battleships had sunk.

I was sobbing uncontrollably. I wanted to tell him right then and there that I was gay. Gay. Gay. Gay. And that was the real reason why I did not want to go back.

"What's eating you up, Jobert?"

"You just don't understand." I wiped tears away with my forearm.

He pursed his lips. He was waiting for a response. But I could tell he was also thinking. Thinking. Thinking. His head drooped slowly forward as he waited for my sobs to subside somewhat.

"Tell you what," he said. "Why don't you audit classes at U.P. for a semester? If you really don't like them, then we'll consider Michigan."

I looked up in disbelief, stifling more tears. That totally made sense. I could attend classes in June and finish a full semester before transferring. A smile started to form inside my chest. I was careful, though, not to give away the leaps of joy that pounded within.

"Thank you, Tatay."

"You're welcome, Job."

Yet again, Tatay managed to find some sort of compromise. This was his trademark over the years. His reconciliatory essence. Finding a way for opposing parties to meet in the middle. Landing on interim solutions when trying to get to the ultimate goal was not immediately feasible. This was why politicians had turned to him for advice. And why he was good at what he did. This is why his family was intact, despite our nomadic existence and all the missteps along the way.

I shook his hand in my head and called it a truce. I was willing to give U.P. a fair shot. Never mind my ultimate goal remained Michigan.

Tatay and I hardly hugged, although I always kissed him and Mommy good night.

"I love you," he said as he squeezed me even tighter. "I want what's best for you, and I want you to be happy."

"I love you, too," I said, my eyes heavy. "I'm sorry."

I was stuck on what was best vs. what made one happy. Was it one or the other? Why could it not be both?

22

Graduation Night Like No Other

Tokyo, 1982

The protective plastic sheath was sticky to my fingers. It tore apart in slow motion, the scent of newness bursting forth from the navy nylon. Once Mommy had her way with the folds and wrinkles, it was to become my perfectly pressed graduation gown. I stole a minute to try it on.

The mortarboard, snug over my skull, had me giggling before the full-length mirror as I looked more like *The Flying Nun* than I did a member of the National Honor Society or President of the Student Body or even President of the Kanto Plain Interscholastic Student Council.

My smile lines soon faded. My eyes squinted with suspicion. I closed in on the pimpled, lazy-eyed, uneven shouldered me I was now interrogating pore by pore. A three-quarters turn to the left, then to the right, and a jerk step back.

You fucking impostor. The revelation was epiphany-like.

I disrobed and flung the tasseled square off my head and across the room only for it to pierce the rice paper shoji window leaving a torn scar.

No one knew who the real me was. All my efforts to be the perfect son, the envied classmate, the one who cared and the one who could, the guy who dates girls; all elements of one big campaign to divert attention from what was under the surface, to disguise the unsavory truth: I had become a male whore.

I was the cross-cultural, new generation 'call boy' for the world's businessmen, impresarios, and entrepreneurs, all with other lives. Traitors in transit at Tokyo's most prestigious accommodation, a carnal and commercial crossroads I had stumbled upon and cracked the nut on, clients whose libidos I had catered to my entire high school career and received handsome compensation. Never mind the initial impulses, the happenstance that enabled me to fall into and voluntarily pursue this double life. And the men I catered to cared not whether I was underage. It was all hitting me in a way that made me want to scratch at it until it turned raw and bled, to shed my skin, to roll back time, to have a second take on my adolescence.

My classmates smoked and drank. I was certain some did drugs and were having sex with Shinjuku hookers. Their vices were not mine, though I may have very well trumped them all in the end.

And here I was on the eve of a young life's milestone, coming to grim grips with what I had become and having to live with my unseemly reality, my tattered, no, my broken self. Who no longer could hold it all together. And no one but a Leonard in New York City to confide in who might even show a shred of compassion for my own predicament.

I slapped my face and banged my palms against my forehead until I fell to my futon sobbing.

With two weeks left of high school, everything I did took on an extra weight, extra significance of being the last this or last that: last final exam, last Student Council meeting, last term paper; last track meet; last school play performance as Ivan Vassiliyitch Lomov, the hypochondriac groom in Chekov's one act play, *A Marriage Proposal.*

Senioritis had taken on epidemic proportions as most of my classmates dressed down (i.e., necktie-less and blazer-less), sunbathed on the school roof, and even played hooky altogether. Each night I arrived home by ten or eleven, my family believing the end-of-high school party invitations were aplenty, which they were, though I usually made a token appearance before heading to the Imperial Hotel's shopping arcade.

I was back to batting a thousand, able to make eye contact with a hotel guest, negotiate, then rendezvous in his room in a matter of minutes. After all this time, I had decoded if not perfected the mating ritual. As for the money, it was still a motivator but no longer a prerequisite, though most of the time, it was thrust into my hand or pocket as I dressed and departed. And I obliged.

Sated, I stared at the subway train's putty linoleum floor all the way home, or at the advertisements above for Pocari Sweat sports drink, the latest gossip rag or manga, the next big JAL summer destination, playing back every lurid act, every tingling sensation, every gratification. I had given up on trying to hold on to names and phone numbers hastily scribbled on hotel stationery, not to mention the empty 'see you next times.' The faces melded, as did their naked bodies, and by most mornings, had melted away from my memory. And I was left empty.

My classmates elected me to give the class speech, to encapsulate our collective experiences and hopes through this rite of passage to life beyond St. Mary's. Determined to say thoughtful things that were to leave a lasting impression, I turned to Tatay to help me shape my themes and tighten my grammar.

I had already turned to him a month earlier to book his boss, the rector of the United Nations University, to be the guest dignitary who would spew wisdom in his address to us graduates. Even after repeated rehearsing of my speech, I was still not sure whether the audience would be wowed, so I added a short paragraph at the end in Japanese, a rehash of how appreciative we all were of those who had supported us on our journey. I passed it by the Japanese language teaching staff for accuracy and proper delivery.

On June 6th, Graduation Day, a heat wave hit Tokyo. I arrived in the gym at 4:30, a couple of hours before the evening ceremony. I felt the power of the podium as I scanned the rows of folding chairs still being arranged by the janitorial staff. Industrial strength fans swirled the stale air, mixed in with chlorine coming through the air ducts from the adjacent swimming pool.

I laid my three-piece navy suit, along with my graduation gown, in the lounge by Mr. Hauet's office and headed outside to sit in the sunken courtyard to face the very last sunset of my high school days. Wondering where all the time had gone. Wandering into where life might take me next.

As we marched down the center aisle to the school band's *Pomp & Circumstance*, I saw my family waving and taking pictures. Mommy's orchid corsage, pinned to her ivory silk dress, was as big as her beaming and already watery eyes. Tatay was all smiles as well, opting for a formal Filipino Barong dress shirt, clasping his hands and shaking them champion-style. Sweat and heat caused itching all across my back. The ceremony for the most part remained a blur, but I read my speech with finger to text, emphasis on underlined words just as I had rehearsed, eye contact across the gym. There was the speech I had prepared and the speech I wanted to deliver.

Good evening Brother Andrew (headmaster), *Brother John* (principal), *Mr. Soedjatmoko* (President, United Nations University), *beloved faculty, parents and friends. Thank you for sharing this memorable evening with us.*

You all are fools. Standing before you is not the real Jobert. You've come to believe I am the ambitious, congenial, dedicated, straight even happy-go-lucky big man on campus who has excelled in academics and athletics. Who has led the student body with aplomb. Well, the truth is that I am gay. And more than that, I am a whore. You heard me right. Throughout these past four years, I have been selling sexual favors to men in the shopping arcade of the fucking Imperial Hotel.

They come from the world over, horny, far from familiar and watchful eyes, seeking carnal pleasure and instant gratification. Even taking advantage of the underaged, the naïve. But that is not me. I always know what I want and how to get it. And be compensated for it. You see this body? My youth? It is the precious commodity they desire.

I have successfully juggled diametrically opposing forces of boy wonder and boy toy, certain that if exposed, it would devastate those of you who groomed me for greatness. And I almost got away with it.

We have learned that education is a life-long process that builds on the knowledge and wisdom of the past; ideally, it should be pursued in all aspects of our daily experience.

I have learned that to be gay at St. Mary's is to be an outcast. To be ridiculed and belittled. Someone whose presence besmirches these hallowed halls. And with no one to confide in, to be my true self with, is it any surprise I have found refuge in the arms of strangers lustful if not lascivious?

We, the members of the Class of 1982, thank our parents tonight, knowing that we can never thank them enough for all the love and care they have given us until now; they made it possible for us to be here.

Tatay, Mommy, thank you for loving me. You have provided me the best upbringing, the best education, the best life experiences. But now I must set the record straight. To faculty and classmates, I must come clean.

I am a homosexual. I like boys. I want to be with men. That is when I am most alive.

And I am deeply sorry to fall short of your expectations.

My speech on how St. Mary's has prepared us for the global village of today and tomorrow was met with thunderous applause. I knew I had delivered on what was expected of me by my classmates, faculty, family and friends. I could claim victory for having walked the tightrope of this double life I had balanced all throughout high school. I had covered my tracks, and no one was the wiser. And I could move on in life unscathed, with my own hard-earned spending money. And regrets along the way.

When all sixty-six of us had our diplomas in hand, we were asked to stand. Brother Andrew blew into the microphone before making his proclamation.

"I introduce to you the newly graduated class of 1982. Congratulations, gentlemen."

In the roar of applause were yells and whistles as well as more flashbulbs and hugs among fellow classmates.

I kept my mortarboard on, but others had already thrown theirs in the air, some like Frisbees to the far reaches of the ceiling and out onto the bleachers in the balcony. Not wanting to be out of step with tradition, I dropped mine behind on my seat, not knowing then that Mommy would keep it for years, along with my gown, not unlike how a bride might keep her dress to mark the occasion.

I was a subway ride behind most of my class, headed to the Roppongi party district for a pre-arranged post-graduation party. I was in my suit sans the medals I received for Student Council President, class speaker, the Japanese language award and a newly instituted Brother Benoit Lessard Service Award named after one of the teachers who had recently passed away—and who would one day be accused of sexual molestation by several students, sending shock waves across the St. Mary's community. These I had left with my parents along with the multiple fountain pens as well as a dozen or more custom-dyed roses— aubergine, indigo, mandarin, fuchsia, all the rage in Tokyo—I had received from girls of sister schools including my prom dates, Yoshiko and Masako, both still weary of the other.

In what was by now an abbreviated conversation with my addicted self, I decided to stay on the subway past the Roppongi stop before exiting at Hibiya and heading toward the Imperial Hotel. After all, the partying was supposed to last until five in the morning. I would get to Phoenix Disco just as everyone was bopping full force on the dance floor and the alcohol was flowing, before it was time for one last bleary-eyed gyudon beef bowl for breakfast in Shibuya.

At just past eleven, the lights had been dimmed throughout the shopping arcade. The display windows were dark, their merchandise barely visible, and I was able to follow my faint reflection as I walked by. Even the classical Muzak which set the mood during the day was hardly audible. The hum that emanated from each emergency exit sign I passed had a sizzle.

As luck would have it, I was not the only one pretending to check out what merchandise was on display by gluing my face against the cold glass surface. Two foreigners and a local I didn't recognize seemed to be engaged in a similar waltz. I was buzzed by the Asti Spumante which I was surprised to see served at the school reception. Tatay had encouraged me to have a few sips, which turned into two glasses albeit from shallow champagne coupes. I was also high on the possibility of consummating the evening with naked fun. Perhaps for one last time. After all, I was done with high school. And as far as I was concerned, at eighteen, I was a full-fledged adult.

The tallest of the three had wavy brown hair and was also in a suit. I was guessing he was an American in his forties. He made a beeline for me. A bit brazen, but then it was late. The pickings were slim. And I was horny.

"Care to join us?" he asked. The other two kept track of our conversation from their separate vantage points.

"All three of you?" I asked.

"Oh, no. Him, that one over there." He nodded to the other foreigner, maybe ten years younger, in jeans and a white-collar shirt. "Forget the Jap. He's been following us all night. Thinks he's gonna get some action. You, we want."

The derogatory term, so backwardly World War II, surprised me but then so did the proposition of going to bed with two men who happened to be a couple. Friends? Lovers? Part of me was dumbfounded, and the other gleeful I was about to add a three-way to my sexual repertoire.

Not much more was said as I followed my two hosts into an elevator up to room 2625. Neither of them touched on the subject of money. This was not the night for it anyway.

There was an elegance to the turned down king-sized bed with chocolate mints, soft Muzak and dimmed lights. The sheer drapes camouflaged a twinkle-lit Tokyo cityscape.

The man who propositioned me wasted no time coming from behind to kiss my neck and blow gently into my ear. I closed my eyes to focus on the warmth of his breath. He then grabbed my stomach with both his hands before untucking my shirt and reaching from below up past my undershirt to search for my nipples, already perked up as he pinched them. I twisted my head to kiss him, his breath still sweet with sake. The other came around to loosen my tie and unleash my belt buckle. My pants fell down around my ankles. He slowly slid my briefs below my kneecaps. A velvety, moist warmth engulfed my dick, my lips still locked onto the other's, our tongues invading each other's mouths in sword-like motions.

There was a fluidity and intensity in a threesome which I had never experienced one-on-one. Was I submerged in the embrace of a boiling public onsen *bath*? Afloat off the coast of Santorini in the Aegean Sea? Or awash by the gentle waves that lapped onto the sugar white sands of Palawan back in the Philippines? All I knew was I was in some sexual paradise, bathed in attention and worship, and I was drowning in ecstasy. Did it get any better than this?

It was 1:55, according to my Seiko. My hosts were fast asleep. I hastily put my clothes back on, thinking I'd grab a cab. In fifteen minutes, I would make a grand and fashionably late entrance at the party. I'd be among friend classmates, many of whom I was sure were inebriated, and many I'd never see again. My evening would be complete if not perfect: graduation, accolades, parental pride, sex, partying, and sentimental farewells.

Just as the elevator opened onto the lobby, I was met by two men, black necktie and suited clones, both of them with walkie-talkies in hand, both sporting the imperial sixteen-petalled chrysanthemum lapel pins.

They asked me in Japanese to please follow them.

"I'm sorry, I have to return to a party," I replied in English as I tried to walk toward the front exit.

They both ran ahead of me to build a human wall in my path.

"Pu-reez dis way." One of them motioned for me to head toward a door next to reception.

Shit. Never have I ever had to contend with hotel security. What did they want from me tonight of all nights? And after all these years?

"I was just leaving from dinner with friends. I am not a thief. Check my pockets."

One of them called into his walkie-talkie and was asked from the other end to await further instructions. We were at a non-verbal standoff with no one else in sight except for more security standing at the hotel entrance.

I sighed. My head was racing for recourse. *What next? What to say? What to do?* For a moment, I thought of making a run for it, thought that was bound to make the situation worse.

"I want to see the hotel manager," I said with indignation. "I want to see him now."

I mouthed in prayer for God, Jesus, whoever was available, to get me out of this predicament as I headed toward the door to which I was being escorted.

Fuck. Fuck. Fuck. Fuck!

They motioned me into a seat in a small conference room, dead quiet and overly air-conditioned. I was shivering although I may have very well been trembling. I closed my eyes and tried to remain calm on the outside, but my mind raced, panic stirring inside of me.

My luck had finally run out. Perhaps it was always a matter of time before the hotel staff would eventually catch up with me. Did anyone really get away with it in the end? Apparently not.

Game over.

Ten, fifteen, thirty minutes had gone by? A plot in snapshots flashed before me: Handcuffs. The police. Escort home. Knock at door. Mommy and Tatay in hastily donned robes, apologizing for the trouble I have caused. Me heading into my bedroom, not uttering a word, packing a bag for an escape to destination yet unknown before their shame turned to wrath.

The knock on the door snapped me back into reality. Another chrysanthemum-pinned man in a suit peeked in, then entered. He greeted me with "konbanwa," a polite good evening. I responded back with a head nod, trying not to make too much eye contact. There was a person-in-charge air about him. He seemed not quite Japanese. Not completely gaijin either. Hafu perhaps. He was slim and boyish. Delicately handsome. He sat across from me. He did not introduce himself.

"Abu-eba, san, so you are a student at St. Mary's International School?" he asked in somewhat fluent English. He looked down at my school ID in his hands. I had handed it over to security.

"I graduated tonight. I'm leaving Japan next week for good." I would start to audit classes at U.P. in a just over a week before my father and I revisited our truce and determined whether I was to stay or head to Michigan. At this point, I might as well have expedited my exit out of Japan, wanting this interrogation to end before it went any further. I was scripting my vow never to return to the Imperial Hotel if I got out of this situation unscathed.

"And your father is with United Nations University?" This time, he looked at my father's business card, which I had handed over as well hoping any diplomatic immunity would instantly extend to me.

He sighed. "You will leave Tokyo soon you say?"

"Yes, and not returning to Japan. Ever."

"I see." He tapped both my ID and Tatay's business card on the table.

"You promise to never return to Imperial Hotel?"

I looked right back at him and into his black pool eyes. "Promise. You have my word. I'm done here, I mean I am going away to college."

"You understand me?" His voice turned stern. "It is not safe to be hanging around here."

"Yes. Yes." I nodded tremor-like, with my eyes shut.

"You should go home now."

With that, he just stood up and handed me my ID and the business card.

"Good luck. Please be safe."

I bowed, averting eye contact. "Thank you. Thank you."

My heart thumped as he opened the door and mumbled something to the men with walkie-talkies stationed outside.

Without words, I was ushered through a side entrance of the hotel that they had to unlock. I did not look back as I walked quickly, without a sense of direction. Even with my release and relief, my heart beat faster. It was now racing as I speed walked and burst into tears. I sprinted in my leather shoes. Through the discomfort, I seemed to run faster than I ever had in any race, headed down the block and around a corner, no one to chase or cheer me on. Breathless, I came toward a trash can and before I could reach for it, I vomited on the sidewalk. It was a full-on cough attack as I tried to catch my breath. I turned away and tried to calm myself down, hunched over, palms to my knees. I wiped my mouth with the arm of my suit jacket. I was left sweaty, chilled, and dizzy.

I let out a laugh. And a howl of sorts. I shook my head to exorcise whatever had just transpired. Tonight. And throughout all the hours and days I hung out in and around the Imperial Hotel. I murmured, "thank you" repeatedly, to God, to Jesus, to whoever, then fell back into audible sobs. The nearby traffic light switched from green to yellow to red and back again without a car or person in sight. I leaned back against the closest building wall, cold marble, and slowly sunk into a squat, waiting for my breath to slow down. I blankly stared at the pavement thinking I was a cat who had just used up one if not more of its nine lives.

By the time the taxi dropped me off at the Phoenix Disco, my heart was back to its steady rate. My eyes were still moist, and I was depleted of adrenaline. I recognized the thumping upbeats of Hall and Oates's "You Make My Dreams" from within. I had yet to know how its melody, its lyrics, would become a timestamp, a trigger, a tribute to my tumultuous Tokyo teens, and the wistful smile it would elicit from me for decades to come every time it played.

I approached the entrance, where I flashed my school ID before the bouncer pulled the door open. I was drawn in by the blast of dancing spotlights and mirror balls, the dampness of fog and sweat. The bass beat that reverberated off my chest. The dancer silhouettes. My soon to be forever secretive past.

And, boy, was I ready to celebrate.

23
Arrival at Departure

Tokyo/Narita, 1982

"Hold tight to your documents," Mommy said, to which I rolled my eyes.

It would have been easy to have an outburst, but I bit my tongue instead, knowing that freedom from filial forces was just minutes away once I waved goodbye to my parents before passing through Immigration.

Except for reciting the rosary as we left the house and our Den-en-chōfu neighborhood, the three of us were silent during the over two-hour drive to Narita, traffic snaking out of Tokyo. It was just ahead of the August *Obon* Festival when folks returned to their hometowns to reunite with relatives and honor the ancestral spirits with altar offerings and grave cleansings. I could not help but think our expedition was the opposite of a homecoming, though the blast of the AC was indeed a blessing under a blue-absent sky, syruped with heat and humidity, notorious this time of year.

The scenery shifted from concrete jungle to jade rice fields and distant undulating hills along the Shin-Kūkō (New Airport) Expressway. As we neared, we were mired in long security checkpoint lines. Concrete watch towers like maximum security prisons menaced us overhead as opaque high metal fencing barricaded any view of the terminals or tarmac. Rural folks remained resistant and even rebellious four years after the controversial opening of the New Tokyo International Airport. And every precaution since day one was intact.

One look at our blue diplomat license plates, and we were whisked through by white gloves and a tip of the hat by police backed by the military might of uniformed soldiers.

Tatay insisted just days ago, after we returned from Manila sans siblings still summering there, that we not part ways at T-CAT, the Tokyo City Air Terminal, located at the capital's core. From there I could have easily checked in, hopped on a bus, got off at the designated departure terminal, and walked straight to security unencumbered. And he and Mommy would not have had to take the trek to the airport. But that didn't happen.

We parked the car and rolled my luggage to the North Wing to seek out the Korean Air Lines check-in counter. Mommy, who had negotiated with her travel agent a deep discount economy fare worth preening about, could not help herself. She peered over my shoulder as I presented my plane ticket and passport to the agent. She sighed in relief as my two matching Louis Vuitton wannabe suitcases, which she purchased for this very occasion and helped me pack in all that I would need in my new world, scraped by just shy of the luggage weight maximum. She also asked to reconfirm that my boarding passes were accurate: Narita to Seoul Gimpo, transit onward to New York JFK, with a fuel stop in Anchorage.

This closing of a chapter between my parents and me was inevitable. I knew it would be. Perhaps I even willed it, since turning thirteen, maybe much sooner, knowing for far too long something was different. That *I* was different. Maybe even special. But I would have to leave home to find and understand my true gay self. It would be a few more years, when I was less fearful and more confident of who I was, that I would muster the courage to come out. But certainly not on this day. It would have been unfair, even cruel, to have detonated such a grenade and lobbed it at my parents just to have left them to deal with the rubble of the aftermath.

Even though I had gone through the motions of auditing courses at U.P. for part of June and all of July, all three of us had quietly realized I was destined to be elsewhere, to study abroad, to be an international student as I had been for so long already. To be the global citizen my parents aspired me to become. To leave the proverbial nest, spread my wet, wobbly wings, and find my own way in the wide world.

I had gotten Tatay off my back, perhaps to appease him too, by signing up for courses on "Politics of the Environment" and "Social Change in Philippine Society," both on his recommendation and offered by former faculty colleagues at the Department of Political Science and Public Administration.

I struggled to make sense of the lectures or readings. I really did not share Tatay's academic passions or sense of service to a society still suppressed by martial law. I would probably veer off from any of his preconceived or prescribed paths for me. I had been away from the Philippines for far too long. I had become too otherly to connect to, let alone command, the subject matter as my classmates did. Never mind the professors who promulgated the agenda of a Marcos dictatorship.

The exception was a composition course I sought out, more from instinct than intent, that I had something to say, something to get off my chest. I had not stayed long enough to tell any truths, though I got a good grounding in sentence and paragraph mechanics.

We craned our necks up towards the furious flip-flip-flip of the pre-digital Departure Board. We knew that the moment had finally arrived.

"Call us when you get to Ann Arbor," said Tatay. "And don't forget to write your Mommy."

"I won't."

"Study hard. Make us proud. Eat well," said Mommy.

"I will."

"Thank your Tito Teddy for hosting you," Tatay said. Tito was to be my pit stop in New York City before I headed to Michigan.

"Where's your wallet?" Mommy said.

"It's right here in my coat pocket," I replied, just as I had when she asked the same question before leaving the house. *No eye roll. No outburst.*

Mommy reached over and hugged me. "Don't forget to pray," she whispered into my ear.

A lump in my throat prevented me from answering her, though we locked eyes as she reached over to my face and tucked wisps of my mophead behind my ears. With her thumb, she rubbed what may have been a smudge I did not know was there on the left lens of my eyeglasses.

Tatay and I hugged tight as well. For the first time, I realized I'd overtaken him in physical stature. And I was the one to whisper.

"Thank you."

He patted me on the shoulder two-three-four times before extending a handshake. Instead, I went in for another hug.

Mommy stifled sobs with Kleenex she always had on hand.

I rearranged the strap of my shoulder bag to cut across me like a seatbelt. I nodded. I smiled. I mouthed an inaudible "I love you" to both of them.

I fell into line for the metal detector. Not a long wait but enough for me to glance back a couple of times as Tatay and Mommy stood where I had left them, eye-locked at me, a hint of awe on their faces.

Even after I was patted down by security, and my hand carry X-rayed, and yes, I crossed over the Immigration check threshold, I knew my parents were still standing in place if just for a few more moments before they turned around and headed back home.

I was assaulted by the cacophony of all that surrounded: the echoing bilingual boarding calls; frenzied shopping amidst the sweet scents and ersatz lighting of Duty Free; flocks of Japanese tour groups marching in all directions, members easily identifiable by their matching visors and lapel pins, their eyes glued on guides holding pennant flags. The transient confluence and dispersion of humanity, restless molecules under a microscope, funneling into satellite terminals with tentacles that were gates and gangways feeding into aircraft. The intoxicating aroma of aviation fuel. The high-pitched drone of engines warming up, not unlike when I had first played make believe with my DC-6 model airplane as a child. The "welcome aboard" smiles. The allure of adventure as I settled into my window seat and accepted a hot towel to soothe my flushed face.

So, this is why we travel. Why we depart and why we arrive. And why I must wander. Far away. To leave behind something of self in order to find the entirety of self. To extend into new horizons that exist in the future yet are informed by the past. Even with a map, an itinerary, a destination, details still yet to fill in, the element of surprise lies within that bit of the unknown.

24

Start Spreading the News

New York City, 1982

"Why thank you!" said the jovial Black taxi driver as I handed him a $10 bill on top of the $25 fare from JFK to Tito Teddy's apartment on E. 81st Street closer to First than Second Avenue. "Good luck in America!"

A musical score had resounded in my mind's movie as I soaked in the radiance that was Saturday night Manhattan through the web of cantilever trusses of the 59th Street Bridge. The driver asked whether it was my first time in the city. I was struck by a jolt of déjà vu.

"I was here with my family five years ago," I replied. "I'm now back on my own. Alone. Off to college." My tone was glittered with giddiness.

Gripping my suitcases by the handles, I inhaled the pungency and stale warmth, the thrum of constant urban motion punctuated by sparks of car honks along the avenue. I was so charged with the wattage of anticipation, I beamed a smile up to the sliver of sky which then refracted back and surged through my chest. I took a deep breath followed by a shrug and an audible "ah."

I had returned to NYC.

I was back in the US of A.

I had to make the most of my five nights and four days before flying out of LGA and on to DTW. I first descended a few steps down, got buzzed in, then navigated Tito's narrow ground floor studio apartment which was overwhelmed with kitchen accoutrements that towered ceiling-high. His TV was tuned into PBS, but I would not fully comprehend its highbrow, begathon-billed programming until much later. There were cookbooks on sagging shelves and piles of brittle, yellowed recipes torn out from *The New York Times* laid across what had to be a dining table next to a trundle bed that would jut out just enough for me to sleep alongside, mummy like. Under a floor lamp and its anemic glow, Tito was deep into the next day's Sunday edition, sections scattered about him, oblivious to, perhaps already surrendered to the mix of mildew, mold, and the impending rot that surrounded him.

Tito asked how my flight from Tokyo was and how everyone in the family was doing, and if I wanted to see a Broadway show, we should line up for half-price tickets. "Sure," I responded, then asked to use his phone. He pointed to the rotary dial on the wall next to a refrigerator door plastered with scribbled shopping lists and more *NYT* recipes all held in place by magnets and masking tape.

For years, my parents fondly spoke of Tito's knack for entertaining. "Legendary," they claimed. His culinary skills, his wizardry in pulling off five-course candlelight dinners for eight or ten, even twelve guests lasting late into the night in this very space. If I was lucky, I might yuk it up with Lauren Bacall or Jacqueline Onassis or some U.N. Ambassador or Oscar-winning film documentarian after they had cocktails in the laundry room across the hall. This most unlikely of private party venues was a high society secret. But a quick take at the two-range electric oven and non-existent counter space, *is that a cockroach scurrying across?*, and back to the length of this sardine can of a space led me to think otherwise.

I had inferred over time that Tito was gay. Nary a mention of any attachment or relationship status. Relatives had described him a bon vivant, a dandy, who spent his money faster than he could earn it. He even may have been borderline eccentric, the running joke being that the characteristic was inherent in the Abueva genes and none of us were immune. In his case, the hearsay seemed infallible: he had had a full ride scholarship to Harvard to study History of Art but dropped out halfway through, opting to retrace the trails of Alexander the Great before landing in Paris to fall in love with food, wine, and the lush life.

He was the closest relative I could have confided in, to whom I could have come out of the closet. But not at that moment. It would be a few summers more before I would do so, and he would claim he always knew.

I dialed the number I'd kept folded in my wallet all summer long. I stretched the long curly cord into the confines of a cramped mothball-scented bathroom with dress shirts and blazers and sports jackets and overcoats that fought for space on a rod over and across the unusable bathtub. I found it to be both ingenious and disturbing. There was a pink sink with a mirror above it and big bright bulbs not unlike those used for makeup backstage. It was just past midnight. I closed the door and stared at my reflection as I sat on the lid of the toilet seat with world map wallpaper behind me, ready for my closeup as connecting clicks soon turned into a double ringing tone in the receiver.

"Hello, Leonard? Jobert here. Guess what? I'm in New York!"

There was a pause. I imagined his pulling on a metal cord to turn on his bedside lamp, his grimaced glance at an alarm clock, then sitting up groggy but straight.

"Jobert! Hello. Welcome! Great, glad you made it."

I was relieved to recognize Leonard's Southern drawl. He had mailed me the right phone number after all in his congratulatory note upon my graduation.

"Sorry to call so late. I wanted to let you know as soon as I got here."

"And you have. So, are you free tomorrow night?"

I had to wait another three days, a Tuesday, before I was able to meet up with Leonard. I went to a prearranged Sunday dinner at my cousin Veda's home on the corner of East 74th and Lexington. She had travelled from Manila to the East Coast to attend Hunter College the same year Tatay and Lanelle spent in New Haven. She stayed on to start her own American story which included her Polish-American husband, Tom, and two children, the boy at Trinity and the girl at The Brearley School.

I was welcomed with a pot roast, potatoes, and my first encounter with asparagus and its accompanying after-dinner alchemy. There was homemade apple pie a la mode, a first for me, as well as seconds.

"Are you ready for your freshman fifteen?" Veda asked as Tom laughed along. The food portions on my plate were a good indicator that I would gain as many pounds in my first year in college.

I badger-quizzed them on the New York City subway system as I tried to grasp the logic of letters vs. numbers, green vs. red, deciphering the most direct route to Washington Square Park close to where Leonard lived. Veda handed me a plastic packet of subway tokens with Y-holes in them and said they should last me while I was in town.

"But beware of pickpockets," she added.

Tito Teddy took me on his version of a crash course to finding my way around the island. We had a croissant and a cup of coffee at the MOMA café.

We checked out what was on exhibit at The Asia Society, the Met, and the Guggenheim.

Then there were the department stores he called "retail temples" with their dazzling displays and overwhelming selections of merchandise, larger than those of Tokyo which were already impressive to begin with. The sprawling men's floors became the flip switch to what would be my future flair for fashion and sense of style. Bloomingdale's, Barneys, Bergdorf Goodman, and B. Altman's. Saks, Henri Bendel, and Lord & Taylor. Even Gimbels and Alexander's. We whisked through The Cellar on the lower level of Macy's Herald Square where he priced out non-stick pots and pans. Little did I know that six years on I would frequent those hallowed halls to work floors above in the buying offices for men's sportscoats and dress trousers.

Tito pointed to a construction site along Fifth Avenue he said was the original site of Bonwit Teller. It was a skyscraper in the making that was to be Trump Tower. I knew nothing about its namesake then. Never could I have imagined that one day I would enter it, ride up a golden lift, and shake hands with Donald J. Trump. Being a correspondent for *The New York Times*, I would pen his first person puff profile for "The Boss" column in the paper's Workplace section.

We shopped at the Union Square Green Market for vegetables unknown to me—twigs of Brussels sprouts, never-seen-them-so-plump tomatoes that he said came from New Jersey, beets the color of blood soaked into a white tee, and sprigs of what-a-strange-fragrance tarragon. I crossed off items on Tito's shopping list which he said were ingredients for the dinner he would prepare that evening as the private chef of a Lester Wunderman. Only when I eventually made my way into a marketing career would I realize Mr. Wunderman's stature as the father of direct marketing.

Tuesday midafternoon arrived, and I was dressed in an ensemble I had seen on a headless mannequin at Macy's: white board shorts and a pink Lacoste polo. Perhaps I had subconsciously chosen it because of the color's gay connotations. I walked toward the bottom end of Fifth Avenue. Gingko trees lined the sidewalks as did rows of bricks and mortar, much of it I would later learn in real estate parlance to be prewar. The sun and sky were as bright as my mood.

Triumph trumpeted as I walked through Washington Square's marble arch framing the Twin Towers. Leonard's apartment was just a couple of blocks past per his instructions in a follow-up call confirming I was to show up for what he called "cocktail hour."

The shift from the Upper East Side to the energy of Greenwich Village was palpable. It was more to my liking with crowds milling about in various states of dress and undress. Several were seated, chatting, cordoning the fountain at the square's center. Others were seated, even sleeping on benches, my first closeup encounter with the homeless. Some were sprawled on the grass, soaking up the sun. A few were in a prostrate position as they propped paperbacks on their elbows while others were flat on their backs Savasana-style. Men were huddled around men, transfixed by chessboards grafted onto stone tables. And there were pigeons everywhere. A boy and a girl who threw out breadcrumbs squealed in fear and delight as the "rats with wings" I would later learn, descended en masse.

I gawked at two men throwing Frisbee in frayed denim shorts, both shirtless, with hirsute chests, taut tummies, and broad shoulders. Another man, his well-defined pecs shaved, dressed in onionskin gym shorts and white tube socks up to his knees, glided through the throngs on a kind of roller skate I had never seen before. He was my first rollerblader.

Inhaling all 360-degrees, I exhaled with the epiphany that this was where I belonged, and I had to find my way back. To weave myself into its fabric. To what was undoubtedly the best city in the world.

"Penthouse C."

The doorman pointed to a bank of elevators after calling up to announce my arrival and butchering my name. Each floor on the ride up was a click on a metronome. I'd hand ironed my shirt and shorts and pomaded my hair, sighing relief for having found my way here and on time.

As I stepped off, I turned right to see Leonard's head poking out as if it was afloat at the far end of a long hallway with only a couple of doors between. His salt and pepper wisp, bespectacled freckled face, and mousy moustache were no different from what I remembered back in Tokyo well over a year ago.

"Well, hello there, stranger," he said.

I paced my steps as I stretched a closed smile. *Don't be too eager. Keep it cool. Act like an adult now.*

"Hello stranger," I replied before coming in for a hug which he invited with his outstretched arms.

My gaze widened as I scanned a living space that could fit Tito Teddy's entire studio four or five times over. It represented the affluence I had always associated with the city. Spanned mural windows flanked a glass door, all looking out into a terrace which faced the jutting Twin Towers and all of downtown. To the right was the Chinese silhouette of a black lacquered credenza holding opium pipes, ceramic blue and white signs of the Eastern zodiac, each with a black bent metal stem. I found the dragon in the center between the rat and the horse. I wondered what Leonard's sign was. I briefly studied a colorfully gilded multi-fold screen mounted above. It looked like a scene from *The Tale of Genji*.

Black bulbous ceiling spotlights on the wall bathed three standing buddhas in light. Gold leafed and gemmed, each had its own mudra or hand gesture, as if to bless whoever sat across on the long black leather sectional. A teak coffee table nearby played off the reds in carpet and the room. I could smell a hint of incense in the cooled air.

A calm overcame me, an instant Zen. Leonard had mentioned his shopping expeditions while abroad. I could tell by the inventory of artifacts that filled his abode of his affinity for an Eastern aesthetic, and a proclivity for all things Asian.

"Would you care for some white wine?" he asked as he gestured for me to take a seat.

"Sure! Thanks."

I interpreted his wink before he walked away toward the kitchen as an acknowledgment that while I may have been below the drinking age of twenty, as confirmed by Tito Teddy, Leonard and I were consenting adults, in a private space without the eyes of the law upon us.

Leonard handed me a glass and offered a toast. "Welcome to New York!"

"Thank you. It's so great to be here. Finally!" The chilled and crisp acidity tickled my tongue and throat. "This is really nice," I said. "Where's it from?"

"Let's see here." He picked up the bottle. "A California Zinfandel."

"I like it." As Leonard described the Napa Valley, I realized there were many grape varieties in many wine countries I had yet to discover. Zin would become my go-to social lubricant for the remainder of the '80s and well into the '90s if not into a new millennium before I would settle on a mix of martinis, Manhattans and Malbec. And rosé in the summer.

We talked about graduation. Family. Summer vacation. What I might study at Michigan, which was undecided, though my father strongly suggested economics followed by, quelle surprise, political science. Most of the air time was mine, part excitement, part nerves, and part my not yet mastering the art of give and take in conversation. Leonard seemed genuinely interested in everything I had to say as he also offered up his plans for return trips the following year to Tokyo, Bali, and Penang.

I did not bother to look at my Seiko. The only track of time I noticed was the technicolor hue of streaked clouds out the window to the far right from where I sat. I was well into a generous Zin refill. Having skipped lunch, I felt tingly in my toes and above my eyes.

"Would you like to see the rest of the place?"

"Sure." I took this to be more than just a casual offer of a house tour, a move I had anticipated anyway. Even so, I did want to see how Leonard's taste carried through the rest of the space, in case I someday had a place as spacious and eclectic and luxurious.

"Take your glass with you."

He extended his hand, extracting me from the warm folds of the couch, then guided me past the dining area through a corridor with framed batik block prints on either side, each gallery lit, all of which I hoped to admire later as I followed Leonard to a door at the very end.

The air within was sweeter. Flames flickered through jewel toned glass holders that dotted the entire room. The vertical shades were drawn. A lone torchiere stood on a corner next to a bookshelf wall with space carved out for a desk with a green banker's lamp and a leather work chair. Displayed among art books, both standing and laying, were a Buddha head, a samurai sword, and a collection of celadon vases. There was a Nakamichi stereo system with hypnotic gamelan gongs floating out of speakers on either end. Across were three framed Tibetan mandalas, also gallery lit, separated by doors I surmised to be the bathroom and a closet.

Close to the center was a king-sized bed, more a mattress atop a black platform with a low headboard-cum-shelf and a reading lamp atop. Several silk and batik print pillows, also jewel-toned, had been arranged atop aubergine satin sheets that looked like they were ironed on. It was as if I had entered an inner sanctum, ready to be sacrificed in some sexual ritual.

As I rested my glass on a side table next to the bed, Leonard closed in and offered another hug. This time I did not pull away.

"Would it be okay if I shower first?" I was self-conscious of having not bathed since arriving days ago, given Tito's unusable bathtub and only having splashed water across my face, chest and armpits as part of my morning ablutions.

"Sure, of course," he replied with another wink, as if to confirm my excellent suggestion. He handed me a plush, royal blue towel and washcloth as well as a folded yukata, a cotton kimono that was to serve as a bathrobe. Leonard steered me toward the bathroom with white and black honeycomb floor tiles and white brick tiles for a wall. The fixtures were sparse and all white including a standalone bathtub with webbed feet and a see-through vinyl shower curtain.

The stream of warm water with its rising steam felt good. I peed my first glass of Zin down the drain. With the bar of Ivory soap handed to me, I lathered up my chest, stomach, crotch, and thighs in rapid strokes. I worked on my anus as well when I detected caresses along my back. Leonard had reached in through the curtain to lather from behind. I closed my eyes, slowly rotating my head from side to side, welcoming the sensation that found its way to the small of my back and down to my butt. A squeeze on one cheek, then the other, followed by taps to confirm the firmness of my glutes.

Even before I suggested he join me, he was already stepping into the tub. He wrapped his arms around my abdomen as he squeezed himself against me, his lips momentarily resting on the nape of my neck. There was a slow yet certain arousal from behind and an instant one in front of me.

He slid his hands up to rest on my chest. He made slow circular motions as if both his index fingers were twins walking through unicursal labyrinths with my nipples at the center. He twisted the tips like dials to a delicate instrument, then flicked at their erectness.

My eyes remained shut though my visual field was on overdrive. Slow hands trailed toward my belly button and on down to brush against my pubes. He embraced my midsection with one arm as the other treaded even lower and toward my hard on, his palm giving a double squeeze before he started to push and pull on it.

"Yeah, you like that, huh?" he whispered into my ear.

"I do. Yes, I do."

I let him at it for a few seconds before I grabbed him to stop, fearful I would come too soon.

I turned around to meet his lips, water streaming down our faces, even entering our mouths as our tongues dueled. I had gripped the bar of soap the entire time. He took it from me, crouched down, and kneeled eye to eye with my throbbing dick. He kissed its tip as he lathered up my balls. He then put the head in his mouth before gorging on all of it as he tugged at my scrotum. I pressed my left palm flat against the wall and grabbed on to the curtain with my right hand, careful not to tug too hard as to tear it down.

The last time I came was the night before I left Tokyo, over five days ago, an eighteen-year-old's eternity. It was reason enough for my moans to be clipped as he worked me over, as I built up to a crescendo that drove Leonard to suck me even faster. And he did not let go.

I grabbed onto his skull with both hands as if it was a basketball before a foul shot. I let out an animalistic roar as I convulsed, tiptoeing with every thrust of mine, the valve within releasing what I could not see but knew was streaming out of me. Even as my breathing returned to its regular rhythm and my hardness softened, and I let go of his head, Leonard remained connected to me, as if not wanting to waste whatever last drip of nectar my body had left to give. And I shuddered. It was a far cry from where we had left off in Tokyo.

I startled awake, a moment of disorientation, wondering whether I had slept through the night. I pivoted my head backward to look out the window with its shades drawn open. The Twin Towers' tops were topsy-turvy, red blinking lights at their corners and up the antenna spire to warn airplanes from getting too close. A purplish curtain spanned the sky.

"How're you doing?" Leonard asked, already sitting up in bed with the reading light on as he flipped through a *National Geographic*. A beady-eyed, red-nosed native of Papua New Guinea stared back at me.

I propped my head toward him with my triangle arm.

"I feel fine. What time is it?"

He reached for my free hand and held on to it over his leg, as warm as a mug of morning coffee.

"It's nearly nine. Have time to grab a bite?"

I clutched my stomach at Leonard's suggestion.

"Yes, of course," I replied, satiated in one way but now starved in another.

As I pulled myself out of bed and gathered my clothes, which were strewn across the floor instead of carefully laid on the ottoman like I thought, I pieced together a flashback from not even a couple of hours earlier. I'd finished showering on my own, dried off, and walked back to the room where a grinning

Leonard was on the lounge chair, his yukata wide open, legs apart, stroking his cock. I'd walked over and peeled off my own yukata to then mirror his strokes while standing, drawing his eyes down at my instant stiffness, to which he came in no time. Last I recalled was me sliding next to him under the sheets. I must have dozed off as he big spooned me.

A balmy breeze greeted us as we walked out the building. The doorman did a double take before offering a knowing nod and a "Good Evening, Mr. C_____." The day's warmth, captured and stored by the sidewalks, crept up my legs. We walked along Thompson Street and took a right on Bleecker where we merged into a confluence of heavy foot traffic, though our pace was out of step with everyone else easily overtaking us from behind or sidestepping us from in front. On both sides of the street were restaurants as well as bars, liquor shops, and what I would come to know as bodegas. I even figured out an awninged entrance to be that of a comedy club we were being wooed to enter with a "first drink free" shout.

Leonard pointed to a corner trattoria with outdoor seating, then he waved to a man in all black. The two top buttons of his dress shirt were open at the top to show a black forest of chest hairs laced with a thick gold chain. Menus in hand, he waved back and pointed us to an open table which allowed us to watch the world go by. Leonard shook hands and exchanged pleasantries.

"Luigi, this is my friend, Jobert. He just arrived from Tokyo."

"Won-der-ful, won-der-ful. Wel-come to A-me-ri-ca." He reached out to shake my hand with his firm grip and sausage fingers. I cringed at the way he greeted me. While friendly, it suggested I might not be familiar with the English language.

I trusted Leonard to order anything off the menu or from whatever specials were mentioned as I said I had no dietary restrictions and I would rather people-watch than focus on the way too many selections to choose from.

It was a night of more firsts. We started off with Italian Wedding Soup, an odd name. I had not asked why it was called that. Moreover, the concept of marriage was nowhere on my radar. Its mini meatballs were mixed with greens in a warm, sweet broth. I wiped the sweat off my brow before turning to risotto. I was surprised to learn how many kinds of rice there were. I became an instant fan of its consistency and creamlike texture and would often order it whenever I went out for Italian.

Our conversation moved to the rest of my time in Manhattan.

"So, will you have time to see any shows while in town?" he asked.

"My uncle says I should see a matinee tomorrow and line up for discount tickets. Any suggestions?"

Tito had been pushing for me to see a show before I left, to which Leonard suggested a show he had tickets for the following night, Wednesday. He then asked whether I might already have plans.

"I'm free." I immediately offered, not knowing what Tito might have had already planned.

"Then it's settled. Seven thirty tomorrow." Leonard asked Luigi for pen and paper then wrote down "Little Theater, West 44th Street between 7th and 8th Avenue."

I did not even ask what we were going to see.

As Leonard settled the bill, a breeze caused the leaves of the nearby trees to rustle. It mixed well with the hum of the crowds and the heartbeat of the city. I had not known precisely at the start how the evening would unfold, though it felt as close to whatever the definition of a perfect evening might be. I did not think I was in love with him. Not according to the definitions I had furtively researched in the school library or conjured up in my head. And there were not the kind of sparks which supposedly went past a sexual encounter. But he was good to me and accepted me for who I was, despite our age difference. And there was great conversation, some fun, tipsiness, this summer evening, and had I already mentioned, New York City?

25
All the World's a Stage

New York City, 1982

"So, who's taking you to see a show?" Tito Teddy asked rather sing-songy, as he served a late lunch gazpacho before heading to dinner duties and I down to Broadway.

"My classmate from Tokyo. His family lives here."

Tito returned a smirk when I told him the show was at the Little Theater, but at least his interrogation ceased.

"I'll still be up past midnight," he said. I did not think much of this.

"My flight's not until 1 p.m. even if I get home late."

"I should still be up when you get home. And we should have breakfast before you go."

"Okay, but please don't wait up for me." I was anticipating Leonard would invite me back to his place, with all that it implied.

I was caught up in an ant colony that rushed down the steps of the 86th Street subway stop to hop on the Lexington Avenue line, its cars graffitied with cryptic scripts and squiggles, the showy markings of artists akin to a dog marking its territory. The ride was a deafening squawk of squeals along the track. I white-knuckle grabbed onto a metal handle to steady myself as best I could all the way to Grand Central Station. I desperately wanted to clothespin my nose to the brew of B.O. that did not seem to faze others around me. Tito suggested I wear my black leather shoes, grey slacks, a white collar shirt, and a blazer. The blazer I hooked off my finger and down my left shoulder. I shed it after emerging onto a sweltering 42nd Street, my eyes squinting as much from the stinging sweat as the sun-speckled windows of the buildings high above. I figured out which way was west. Tito instructed me to turn right on Broadway and insisted I stay between Broadway and Seventh Avenue until I got to 44th Street. I was also to keep my wallet in my front pants pocket. He had triple-threatened me with lurking dangers of drugs, deceit, and death. And I was not to linger afterward. I was to hail down the first cab possible for a ride back to a safer Upper East Side.

I was a good hour ahead of my scheduled rendezvous with Leonard. Further down 42nd Street past Seventh Avenue were a cluster of theaters on either end with marquees jutting out in diagonals over the wide sidewalks. Many were blazoned in big black type as if on the lines of sheet music: XXXs and titles like *Fallen Angel, Teenage Pajama Party, Hard Candy* and *Baby Cakes*. I instinctively knew these to be dirty movies. As if pulled by the stretch's magnetic field, I bypassed both Broadway and Seventh Avenue and continued down the northside past storefronts with more XXXs, this time in neon, touting "Live Girls" and "Videos." My imagination was ablaze as I walked past these establishments along with those for peep shows and massage parlors. I gawked at a movie poster of a woman with two blimps for breasts.

I rubbernecked whichever entrances were propped open and the hard-to-decipher dark interiors from which men darted in and out. My nose flared at the stench of urine which had something sharper to it, even intoxicating, reminiscent of paint thinner. In a couple of years, I would know it as poppers, isopropyl nitrate, inhaled for a quick high and in part to relax one's oral and anal muscles.

Trash swirled, billowing into tornadoes caused by what little breeze had stepped out into the evening. Even in broad daylight, the tenor of the block was unlike any other I had walked through in Manhattan. The sun was blotted out. It was dim and dingy, reeking of desolation and decay. It would be best described by a slew of synonyms I would acquire over time as I Americanized: seedy, seamy, sleazy, sordid, salacious. Even titillating. Pagodas of temptation as far as my eye could see.

I wondered whether any establishments offered films of men getting it on with other men, like the ones Leonard had described back at the Imperial Hotel. It would be three summers into the future, during my internship at the fare desk of Japan Air Lines on Fifth Avenue, that I would discover the ease of walking through any of these doors to hit the jackpot of VHSs and magazines catering to a man-on-man audience.

Under one of the marquees, next to a box office with an attendant dozing off, a tall, Black woman in a blonde wig and silver platform boots, tight lime green skirt, and shaggy white coat just down to her belly button whistled my way.

"Hey, honey! Do you have the time?"

I did not turn. She may have been calling out to any of the other men walking by.

Not quite to the end of the block which I presumed to be Eighth Avenue, I made a U-turn and picked up my pace.

"Honey, don't be afraid. I do bite." A deep cackle followed.

I wanted to run but knew better not to. I was still unfamiliar with the connotation of a city's underbelly though this was the scene that my future mind would reference whenever I or another spoke of one.

My inhalations and exhalations moderated as soon as I turned onto Seventh Avenue. I let out a deep sigh, relieved at how quickly the world turned to brightness and a bustling of humanity. It was as if I had just clawed my way back from a fall off the earth's edge.

It was still early when I got to the Little Theater, which was playing a show called *Harvey Fierstein's Torch Song Trilogy*. I killed time, propelled by throngs up and down Seventh Avenue and Broadway. I came across the TKTS booth Tito kept referring to as where I was to line up for half-priced tickets. I walked by the theater for *A Chorus Line* which I had seen with family three summers ago. The struggle to make it as a dancer, as a performer, as a gay man had left an indelible imprint, and I returned to fighting back tears when the cast danced and sang to "One." And for a moment, I wished I was seeing the show again to relive the melancholy and ache of really wanting something more than anything else in the world. I also walked past a show with a curious title: *The Best Little Whorehouse in Texas*.

Back at the Little Theater around 7:15, I stood at the curb and waited, steering clear of theatergoers as they scurried in all directions to their designated shows. Leonard tapped my shoulder from behind just after 7:40. He, too, was in grey trousers, a white dress shirt, and a blue blazer. He wore a sweet aftershave: Drakkar Noir. I remembered having dabbed it onto my pulse points after showering at his place.

"Well, look at you," he said.

We laughed at the coincidence of our coordinated outfits. With our age and physical differences, we would not have been mistaken for twins, let alone relatives, but perhaps for something else entirely.

Leonard was handed our playbills, and the usher pointed to seats smack in the middle of Row J. It was a full house with mostly men in the audience. I was stone faced to the wide grins and intense gazes of those directly behind, as if they knew something about us. Leonard paid no heed as he flipped through his playbill.

He asked what I did today.

"I just walked around," I replied.

Our small talk included him having conference calls with South America and planning for his return there. I wanted to ask him what the show was about just as the lights dimmed.

How did four hours fly by and time still feel as if it stood still? I was transfixed, confused, and bewildered by all that was happening on stage starting with it being a play and not a musical as the title suggested though there was singing by a lady blues character next to a piano between acts.

I was unable to keep up with many of the jokes, although I found it particularly funny when the main character, Arnold Beckhoff, in his silk kimono, exaggeratedly fluffed the many bunny-shaped pillows on his couch. My eighteen-year-old self couldn't get all the soliloquys and fast-paced dialogue being lobbed like snowballs to my chest. I was taken by their force, puzzled why I sensed I was being spoken to directly, unable to regain my composure before the next one squarely struck me.

The three acts assaulted me with sexual innuendo and melodrama, an existence both foreign and familiar: disillusionment over love, a Jewish gay identity and Yiddish slang, drag queens, bisexuality, anonymous backroom sex, gay adoption, and gay marriage. A porridge of identities and issues that would play out in society and throughout my lifetime. But on this day, in a single seating, I was receiving a crash course complete with the *Cliff Notes* of New York City Homosexuality 101.

Of all the characters, I instantly related to Alan, who was my age. He aspired to be an actor while working as a model. He was a hustler, making money selling sex like I'd done back in Tokyo. I saw fact playing out as fiction up on stage although the plot diverged when Arnold and Alan fell in love and considered starting a family, neither of which shone a light in my own universe.

And I could not help but intuit it was no accident Leonard had brought me to see this show. That these top-priced tickets for orchestra seats happened to be available for my last night in Manhattan. That he must have planned for us to see it together once he confirmed I was in town. I worked myself up into a frenzy as to whether he was setting me up for the possibility of more between the two of us after the carnal fun of the night before.

Alan got ambushed by a group of boys who called him a faggot as they chased, kicked and bludgeoned him until he was lifeless. The brutal attack, punctuated by the suggested siren lights bathing the stage, cast an eclipse on my entire being as well as a throbbing of my forehead. It was as if I had arrived at the dark side of this new world I sought to be a part of where, here in America, there was more freedom to be who I truly was yet where gays were hated and victimized. Perhaps this path was too treacherous after all. AIDS. Being called a fag. Facing constant ridicule. Yes, even disappointing my parents. And now gay bashing. It was enough to make me want to recoil into the safety of the closet, wishing I could have switched up the past with Merethe, Piyun, and Yoshiko. And to have Stephen, Robert, Lars, Curt and whoever else recede into the fold. I would be more alert to any limping of my wrist or any fey to my manner here then on out.

Leonard must had seen the shell-shock on my face during both intermissions. I had not said anything, though I'd made hand motions of needing to use the men's room. I found myself in long lines which left little time for us to touch base on what we thought of the show thus far. Toward the end, I found myself among the chorus of sniffles in the dark at Alan's death and Arnold's inconsolability even as he was fathering David, the son he and Alan had wanted together but Alan did not live long enough to meet. I could not control the gushing of my tears throughout the prolonged standing ovation and as the house lights came on.

"Are you all right?" Leonard asked as we found ourselves back on the curb, another balmy night greeting us. It was past midnight.

"Yes. That was quite a play," I replied.

"It certainly was." Leonard had rolled up his playbill into a tight baton, tapping it against his open palm.

"Shall we take a taxi back to my place?" he offered.

"I'd like to, but I fly out tomorrow."

"Oh, are you sure? I could get you a cab after a nightcap."

"Nightcap? A drink?"

Leonard laughed. "Yes, I have some more Zinfandel. It'd be nice to be naked again with you."

"It would be. But my uncle is probably waiting up for me." My mind was still back in the theater, if not right up on stage, playing back scene fragments. I was still trying to digest the entire evening. On any given occasion, I would not have hesitated at an open invitation to have sex. It was the single force to which I had and would continue to succumb. And I would want to thank some force other than God or Jesus, as it seemed inappropriate to hold them accountable for the libidinous appetite with which I have been blessed. But there was this nagging loss of balance, a profound shift in perspective, all because of this one play that caused me to rethink what it meant to be gay and what truly was behind wanting another man's attention and admiration.

"Are you sure now?" Leonard's question turned into a plea.

I sighed. "I am sure. I had a wonderful time. I plan to be back at Christmas time. We can see each other again then?"

It was Leonard's turn to sigh. "Yes, of course. We can meet up again. Call me before you return."

"I will." I said this, knowing full well I wasn't sincere. Something inexplicable had caused the curtain to come down on our whatever it was. What I did know was that I had no interest in being tethered to someone else, let alone tied down. I did not want to be held back by another when my young adult life was about to go into high gear. In a matter of weeks, I would be a changed person with new outlooks and social networks. I would shed my proverbial old skin. The present would become the past, and I was not to make any contact with Leonard ever again.

"Well give me a hug then." Leonard opened his arms to me. I did a quick take of who may have been watching, really no one, before I leaned into him. I did ever so quickly, almost as if under duress and hoping it was enough to count and that I may be excused. Leonard flinched at my awkwardness.

"You take care of yourself, Jobert."

"I will. You as well. Thank you for everything."

I cheesed a smile before I made my way up the blocks toward Tito's place. I was not about to turn around to see Leonard still standing where I had left him. I imagined him watching me drift off and out of his line of sight, hoping for a head turn, like our first chance encounter at the underground shopping arcade of the Imperial Hotel that now seemed like a lifetime ago. And like with all the others, every innuendo, every connection, every conquest, every momentary high, every brittle regret even as I counted up the crisp money bills.

Well, the gamble, it no longer seemed to be in the cards.

Coda

You think to tip the Greyhound driver as he yanks your luggage from the belly of the bus. You decide otherwise, unsure what is customary in the Midwest, in the state of Michigan, in the city of Ann Arbor that is to be your home base for the next four years. You'll love it. You'll loathe it. It's still too soon to tell.

You are an early arrival. It's before Labor Day weekend, the concept of which you have yet to grasp, but you are gung ho to get the lay of the land before a mass migration descends upon campus and the new academic year. You wonder whether a gay bar even exists.

To locate West Quad, you are to look for the Michigan Union to which it is connected. The ivy-infested brick and cement structure of a bygone era belies the pulse of student life within, with which you will become intimate—late night pizzas, study group booths, Mountain Dew runs, friends and foes that have yet to be constructed—a full immersion into the GO BLUE! culture, that by the time you attend your first football home game against Wisconsin, will it run through your veins for eternity.

You stop at the main entrance to catch your breath. You look up to the statues on either side: the buff athlete on the left, facing the stadium, and the garbed scholar on the right examining Angell Hall, where professors will shift your perspective on life, your sense of self.

You close in on the plaque to the left, which notes that John F. Kennedy stood on these very steps, delivering a speech announcing his proposal for the Peace Corps. And the inscription confirms that it happened on October 14, 1960 when he was still a presidential candidate.

You sigh yet again. Perhaps your soul is stirred by your closeness to this commemoration, albeit twenty-two years after the fact. That shouldn't matter. Allow the epiphany to set in deep into your body, your entire being, that you are here, in the now and the new, of your own accord, to think big and become your best self, whichever form it takes.

"How do I get to Adams house?"

The guy behind the desk seems only a couple of years older than you and very much your type—blond, blue-eyed, and chiseled. He points you around the corner and down the stairs toward dark wood double doors with metal bars that lead into a long, glass paneled corridor basked in sunlight, John Cougar's "Jack and Diane" echoing behind them.

"Welcome to the University of Michigan!" His milk white teeth light up as he cheeses widely, wholesome, almost painfully so.

You roll your suitcases toward the front desk and the music. The wheels gliding against brick square tiles reverberate, not unlike a sheet of paper fed into a Smith Corona, cylinder knobs turned by hand until it appears under the guide, locked in place, and the carriage pushed as far to the right as it will go.

That sounds about right. After all, you now have a blank page, ready to type your next chapter. In these United States of America.

Acknowledgments

This book project began at the turn of the millennium when I quit Corporate America and moved from New York City to Bucks County, PA with my then partner Bruce Imber. He was there when the seeds were first planted.

A handful of writing groups over the years read shitty drafts and offered valuable feedback. Thanks to Michael Mele and Linda Mironti of Il Chiostro for offering an online writing workshop during the pandemic which fueled completion of my manuscript; and to Sheila Bender, writing instructor extraordinaire as well as fellow writers: Nancy Conrad, Jaye Moscariello, Rhonda Stanley, Marcella Smith and Andy Holtzman.

This is a story of family and a blessed boyhood. Thank you to my now gone parents, Jose (Pepe) Veloso Abueva and Maria (Coring) Socorro Encarnacion, and to Lanelle, Rossana and Jonas. To Tito Teddy (RIP) as well as my other titos and all my titas, cousins and family friends, maraming salamat po.

Thank you to all my teachers and classmates who had put up with me as I attended the University of the Philippines Child Development Center, Ateneo de Manila, British Primary School in Kathmandu, Ruam Rudee International School in Bangkok, International School in Manila and St. Mary's International School in Tokyo. Special thanks to Mr. Peter Hauet who was the best high school guidance counselor anyone could ever hope for.

I am beyond lucky to have met Ian Henzel and St Sukie de la Croix of Rattling Good Yarns Press while attending Saints & Sinners LGBTQ Literary Festival in New Orleans. Their care and professionalism in shepherding this book into the world has been a gift. Thanks too to Don Weise for structural feedback, and Jerry Wheeler for his editorial eagle eyes and encouragement.

My gratitude to Dennis Bertland, Daniel T. Gramkee and the New Hope Celebrates History Committee for featuring me in their Artists & Authors Speakers Series even before my book was out. Also to Lambda Literary for the honor of being the inaugural recipient of the J. Michael Samuel Prize.

Finally, I am never alone with so many friends, colleagues, and acquaintances old and new, near and far, the world over. Thank you for this abundance in my life.

About the Author

Jobert E. Abueva is winner of the Lambda Literary J. Michael Samuel Prize and Writer's Advice Flash Memoir contest. He is also recipient of the Arch and Bruce Brown Foundation Literary Award for historical LGBTQ short fiction as well as two National Arts Club literary scholarships. His writings have been featured in *The New York Times, The Philadelphia Inquirer, Beyond Queer Words, Harrington Gay Men's Fiction Quarterly* and *Poetry Nippon.* Jobert holds degrees from the University of Michigan – Ann Arbor (BA) and Columbia Business School (MBA). Born in Manila, Philippines, he is a global marketer by day, and resides in New Hope, Pennsylvania. Read more at jobertabueva.net or follow him on Twitter (@jabueva), Facebook (@joberteabueva) and Instagram (@jobert_abueva).